THE
POWER
OF YOUR
WORDS

STEP-BY-STEP GUIDE TO CONFIDENTLY WRITE YOUR BUSINESS BOOK

FIONA MAIRI TAYLOR

Copyright @Fiona Mairi Taylor

ALL RIGHTS RESERVED: No part of this book may be reproduced or transmitted in any form whatsoever, electronic or mechanical, including photocopying, recording, or by any informational storage or retrieval system without the express written, dated, and signed permission from the author.

Author: Fiona Mairi Taylor @2024
Title: The Power of Your Words – Step By Step Guide To Confidently Write Your Business Book

ISBN: 978-1-7384171-1-7
Category: Self-help/Writing/Business/Books
Publisher: Breakfree Forever Publishing

LIMITS OF LIABILITY/DISCLAIMER OF WARRANTY: The author and publisher of this book has used their best efforts in preparing this material. The author and publisher make no representation or warranties with respect to the accuracy, applicability, or completeness of the contents. They disclaim any warranties (expressed or implied), or merchantability for any particular purpose. The author and publishershall in no event be held liable for any loss or other damages, including but not limited to special, incidental, consequential, or other damages. The information presented in this publication is compiled from sources believed to be accurate. However, the publisher assumes no responsibility for errors or omissions. Theinformation in this publication is not intended to replace or substitute professional advice. The author andpublisher specifically disclaim any liability, loss, or risk that is incurred as a consequence, directly or indirectly, of the use and application of any of the contents of this work. Printed in the United Kingdom.

THE
POWER
OF YOUR
WORDS

STEP-BY-STEP GUIDE TO
CONFIDENTLY WRITE
YOUR BUSINESS BOOK

FIONA MAIRI TAYLOR

Breakfree Forever Publishing

*This book is dedicated to John,
the boy with the beautiful smile.*

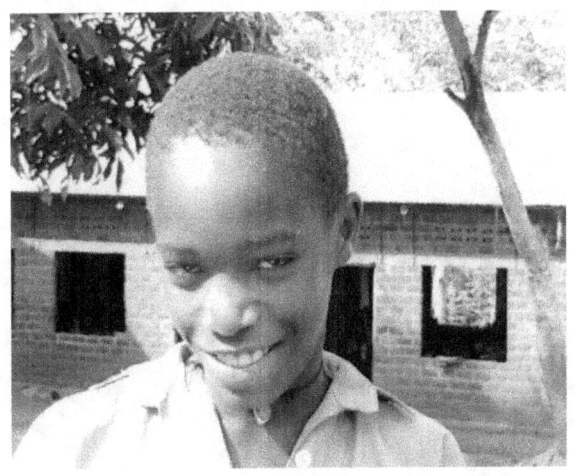

CONTENTS

Prologue 3

PART ONE: THE POWER OF YOUR VOICE — 11

CHAPTER 1 Self 13
CHAPTER 2 Sound 25
CHAPTER 3 Smile 35
CHAPTER 4 Style 45
CHAPTER 5 Spirituality 57
CHAPTER 6 Strength 67
CHAPTER 7 Shine 73
CHAPTER 8 Speak 85
CHAPTER 9 Story 93
CHAPTER 10 Speciality 101

PART TWO: THE POWER OF YOUR WRITTEN WORDS — 111

CHAPTER 1 The Business Book Blueprint 113
CHAPTER 2 B.R.I.D.G.E. 121
CHAPTER 3 Build 125
CHAPTER 4 Recognise 133
CHAPTER 5 Identify 141
CHAPTER 6 Distil 149
CHAPTER 7 Generate 157

CHAPTER 8	Evolve	163
CHAPTER 9	Ways to connect	171

Acknowledgements *175*
Testimonials *177*
The Family *181*

PROLOGUE

It is September 2013, and I am sitting in my office, located in the stunning campus of the University of Stirling, in the heart of Scotland.

The window is open, and I can smell the crisp, clean air with its fresh and invigorating quality, which has taken on a slightly earthy and woody undertone. There is a cosy aroma of wood smoke, with the chrysanthemums and asters adding their perfume too.

Immersed in the tranquil and nostalgic sound of leaves gently rustling along the path and gracefully descending from the trees, I am brought out of my reverie by the resonant honking of geese flying in a V-shaped formation above.

Looking out at the palette of red, orange, yellow and brown transitioning leaves, I can see the rugged outline of the historic, baronial castle. Its reflection growing longer across the lake, as the earth tilts away from the sun and the ubiquitous might of the Wallace Monument, a testament to the great Scottish leader gracing us with its presence on the skyline. It casts a unique and serene atmosphere on the photograph on my desk of John, the last, special child I support in Uganda. He is now 11 years old, smiling positively, dressed in his new school uniform, and exuding the essence of youthful energy and curiosity.

Feeling that enduring sense of love and connection, despite the physical distance, I am interrupted by the entrance of Lesley, the Sarah Davies lookalike whom I admire greatly for her work and support with budding entrepreneurs on the UK TV show, Dragon's Den. Her air of self-confidence and professionalism, plus her physical appearance is impeccable. Every detail is well thought out, projecting an image of strength and competence.

"Hello Fiona. Thank you for seeing me. It was great to meet you at the International Trade Show a few weeks ago. As I said at the time, there is something a little bit delicate that I wanted to talk to you about. My business partner and myself are going through a little bit of rocky patch.

I want to get out of the business, but I don't want to leave without what I believe I am worth. I'd like your help with writing down all the business knowledge that's in my head. And you were talking about how you had written a book.

So, I'm wondering whether you could help me to write a business book. That would get my story and knowledge right out of my head and into intellectual property. This will add value and then we can sell the company. I really could use your advice?"

Have you ever been able to see something so clearly for someone else? Well, that's exactly what was happening here. I discussed with Lesley how to go about getting her knowledge out into intellectual property and we agreed to meet in a few weeks.

"Fiona, I just wanted to show you this now. I think I have the structure right. I have created the business book just as you told me to. I hope I've got the intellectual property right as we're just about to sell the business.

You know, I was wondering, could you and I work together? You have created the editorials, updated all the chapters, and produced additional ones. As I've got to know you, I've realised that you coach similar clients to me, plus with your speech coaching, so there's synergy between us."

I suppose looking back, that is when our business started. Our international coaching co-operative excelled for three years, and it was brilliant. I was able to host international events with guest speakers and we were even developing Educational Tourism – a new concept for people who wanted to go on holiday and learn new things. I was very grateful for the additional income as it meant I could provide more support for the Ugandan charity Bega Kwa Bega, and I was becoming very used to the 'Camilla calls for cash!'

I was regularly speaking at many events about how to use your voice to share your knowledge. Plus, like Lesley, I was working with clients who wanted to learn how to write and publish their business book. My book, *Discover Your Voice of Power* was written and was ready to be published.

Today was another amazing day…

I want you to picture this. I am sitting at the coffee table in my office with Lesley, looking at the enormous trophy I had received. It had a shiny plaque stating, 'Fiona Taylor - Most Impactful New Speaker.'

A huge box of flowers had just arrived, and I was very happy.

Perhaps you can remember a time when you felt recognised and appreciated?

Lesley, sitting opposite me, was about to yell with delight at my gifts, but was abruptly halted by the jarring sound of a mobile phone.

"Wee minute Lesley, oh it's Sister Camilla from Bega Kwa Bega." Laughingly I add, "Probably wanting more money for the children!"

"Good morning, Sister Camila…Sorry, I don't understand. How could this happen? How could John have drowned in a land-locked country? Why did no-one teach him to swim?"

I was heartbroken, overcome with grief. Each tear was a reminder that I would never read more of his adorable, cherished letters and see photographs showing him growing up. It all vanished in a heartbeat.

Have you ever been at the stage where you just thought you were just going through the motions? Have you ever thought you were just sleepwalking through life. I'd love to say it was 40 days in the wilderness, but it was more like four years.

I buried my sadness and delved into my work to stop myself thinking.

Now it's January 2022. It's almost Spring - the season of transformation and optimism, breathing life back into the world. The dormancy of winter left behind and a time of hope, growth, and brighter days ahead.

I am in George Square in Glasgow, a vibrant and inviting space that serves as the heart of the city centre.

I can smell the spring flowers, a fragrant embrace of nature, welcoming you into a world of beauty and renewal and colour.

I can hear a lone piper playing a walking tune, a potent blend of history, culture, and emotion, stirring your heart.

I simply bumped into Lesley standing in front of me.

"Well Fiona, how many books did you finally sell?"

"Well, hello Lesley, nice to see you too. I never published it."

"Fiona, bloody hell! What do you mean you never published it? You had the ISBN number, so you were able to publish. You stood on stage to tell people how easy it was to write books. You helped me to make a lot of money selling my business and writing my book. I thought that dedicating the book to John would drive you to getting it published and with creating sales help the other children. You know, you didn't die Fiona, but it sounds like your dreams did."

There it was – the cold, hard face of reality. The reminder that I had been so buried in my own grief, that I had forgotten the bigger picture of advocating for positive change for the children. I'd forgotten about raising awareness, participating in campaigns, and supporting Bega Kwa Bega towards a better world.

Do you perhaps possess knowledge and skills that could assist others in overcoming their challenges and finding relief from their pain?

I made an immediate decision to complete what I'd started all those years ago. I was not only going to publish my own book, but to help others do the same.

For the next few months, it wasn't easy because people were saying: "oh, you think you are the next JK Rowling? Do you know how many years she was writing books before she got her first break?"

Well, it's a business book. It's learning.

I also experienced a lot of, "So you can teach me how to write a business book in two days?"

I was full of uncertainty because at this stage, even though I had written the book, I hadn't published a book myself, so how could I teach others?

However, little by little, things started to change.

Firstly, I landed a small contract with one of the Scottish local authorities. It was about better writing skills. I couldn't believe it was to talk to small businesses about how to transfer their intrinsic knowledge into print.

Then I won a major contract with one of the international financial institutions, to deliver a coaching/mentoring/training program, from speech and language performance to person-centred leadership and neurodiversity.

I realised, I could help others to share their wisdom and knowledge through the power of their voice, by turning it into the written word to create intellectual property, just as I had done with Lesley and many others.

Now, this book consists of two parts.

The first part is the book I wrote years ago, albeit with some new elements, to help you find even more power in your spoken word.

The second part is of course, how you can use these words to contact even more people that you can help, by writing your business book.

Now, what do I mean by writing your business book? It's taking all the amazing knowledge, experience, and expertise that you already have within you, and that you've been utilising to lead your organisation and putting all that content down in a well-written business book.

But the thing is, why is it important?

Just as a picture frame provides structure and context to showcase a work of art, a business book ensures clarity and coherence. It frames the author's expertise, allows readers to grasp and appreciate the valuable insights within the book. The book frames your knowledge making the content more accessible and engaging.

Now this is important: the Grammar Factory Publishing Company surveyed its authors and discovered that some of their entrepreneur-authors had doubled their earnings since the publication of their business book. In addition, for some entrepreneur-authors 63% were featured on online magazines, 43% in newspapers, 33% on radio and 10% on TV.

So, you may ask what kind of impact will this have on my organisation? Well, this type of exposure in newspapers, magazine, radio, and TV, means that you are seen. This is especially true when your picture is on the front cover of a publication, and results in an increased engagement with your client base. International sports champions such as Ben Ainslie, the world-renowned sailor, is a motivational speaker. Ben helps others with his winning secrets as an Olympic gold medallist. His book title is *Close to the Wind: Britain's Greatest Olympic Sailor*.

Why is this the case? It is because all business owners know, it's not about how many people they know, it's about how many people know them - the simple law of economics.

So, why is it so important to write a business book now?

Some professionals do not take the time to finish their book. However, if you did, it would give you a distinct advantage, because you are demonstrating your commitment and dedication to your field.

There is a global advantage as well. You can share your knowledge and expertise with people from different and diverse backgrounds, and locations.

Today's business trends are evolving, which means making changes, updates, and reviewing the strategies and latest insights to put into your book, so you can end up releasing a version of your book every year. Then it becomes part of one of those profound knowledge libraries that people rely on, a key addition to their business bookshelf.

A published book becomes part of your professional legacy. It can influence and inspire future generation of businesses and business professionals. There is no better way to give back.

Publishers are always on the lookout for fresh perspectives, diverse voices, varied genres, styles, and innovation.

If you have knowledge, ideas and you can speak, then you are already able to help positively change lives.

So, let's begin with Part One – *The Power of Your Voice*, the book that was originally written while John was still alive.

This is followed by Part Two - *The Power of Your Written Words*.

PART ONE
The Power of Your Voice

1 SELF

The 10 best questions to define yourself. Who is the real you in your voice?

'Whatever you can do, or dream you can, begin it. Boldness has genius, power, and magic in it.'

— Goethe

Everybody talks about the way you look and what the car in your driveway says about you. Often it is said, paint a picture, it tells a story, because it paints a thousand words. But nobody ever speaks about how you sound tonight.

As a nation, even as a world, we are obsessed with visuals – everyone sees what make and even what car model is in your driveway, but no one sees how much money is in your bank account. If your trainers already have the seal of approval, that ticks a box, then it says that you are a person that just does it. No memory exists of Newton's law of gravity when the apple fell off the tree. Now, it is a symbol of disposable income and state of the art technology.

So, what of the spoken word? No longer are texts and messages or having sausages for tea, enough. We want to see and hear the person on our screen. People want to be seen and heard, as evidenced by the explosion of videos on YouTube. Even the name dictates that it's about you, so that you can be heard and seen.

We never get a second chance to make that first impression. People decide in 3 seconds if they like you or 8 seconds, looking at the front cover of your book to decide if they will flip over to the back page. Then, they spend only 15 seconds on the back cover to decide whether they want to buy the book.

So, in 3 seconds, people have made the conscious decision to like or not like you. How long do you think it takes for people to decide whether they like the sound of your voice or not?

The answer is also an astounding 3 seconds.

Do you know how you sound?

Would you be able to recognise the sound of your own voice?

I doubt that and I doubt you would too.

The reason I say that is as follows: if you were to record 20 of the closest people you know speaking a simple sentence of 5 words, then magically put the sentence together so that only 5 of the 20 people said one word each, and then played it back, would you be able to recognise the 5 people and identify in the correct order, which word was spoken by whom?

This is a great game to prove the point that we don't know how we sound.

This book will teach you different ways to use your voice to get what you want:

- It not the content of what you say, but the perfection of the delivery, which is the most important attribute
- People want to feel, and not just hear your passion
- The last draft of your talk is always the best, less is often more
- Start talking with identification
- Modelling – vibrato, resonant tone, and good pronunciation
- Quiet strength – lower your voice an octave and be heard louder
- Super confidence – everyone has a right to be confident and successful
- It's your story – make it your own
- Spirituality - the best prayers are the ones you say to yourself
- Sustainability – reinvent yourself and grow rich.

How many times have you thought that you deserved more? You only have one life. Time is your most precious resource. Do you work towards the life you have always dreamed of, or do you simply exist? How many more years do you want to live unfulfilled?

Would you like more money? Would you like more money with less hassle, handing you the time and the lifestyle that you really deserve? Okay, you have heard it all before, but I have empowered more than 40,000 people to use their most valuable free asset, their voice, to create the life they dream of. I know this works and it will work for you.

Our voice dictates how we sound to other people and how much attention they pay to us. This is the way we get our message across and how others relate to us. So, if you suspect that it's not you, but your voice, that is stopping your relationships and romances and even your remuneration, your voice is clearly working against you and devaluing what you are saying.

What does your voice say about you? Is your voice serving you well? Is it a voice of power when it needs to be? Start now, it's never too late to go for a career of success and have a voice that tells the world who you are.

We are all unique and special, but have you ever considered asking yourself what makes you who you are and how you sound? When we were young, we had ambitions and dreams of what we wanted to be when we grew up. So, what happened to those goals and aspirations? Do we simply let life take over, rather than claiming a life of our own with meaning and direction stamped all over it?

To discover your voice of power, you need to know who you are, where you are and where you want to be.

These are the 10 best questions to define yourself when you speak. I have provided example answers to the questions for you and there is space for you to write down your answers.

1. **What defines your character? E.g.**
   a. The way you interact with people
   b. How you come across, how you are seen and how you are judged
   c. How you do anything portrays your character type – seen as a go-getter, party animal, or one who never rocks any boats

Your answers...

a. ....

b. ....

c. ....

2. **What dictates your personality? E.g.**
   a. Your beliefs – what is important to you
   b. How you live your life each day
   c. Being on the journey, living and learning

Your answers...

a. ....

b. ....

c. ....

3. **Why is your identity important? E.g.**
    a. Defines who I am as a person
    b. Let's other people relate to me
    c. Allows other people to mirror my individuality

Your answers...

a. ....

b. ....

c. ....

4. **What does your brand say about you? E.g.**
    a. Makes me stand out from the crowd
    b. Allows other people to see me as the expert
    c. Signifies quality, better than the rest

Your answers...

a. ....

b. ....

c. ....

5. **What is significant about your uniqueness? E.g.**
    a. Accentuates my distinctiveness
    b. Highlights why people would buy or deal with me
    c. Emphasises that I am a one-off, not a clone

Your answers...

a. ....

b. ....

c. ....

6. **What portrays your sexuality? E.g.**
    a. Dress code – for effect, feminine or masculine
    b. Body language – James Bond, Cynthia Rabbit
    c. Speaking tones – Rocky, Anna in Frozen

Your answers...

a. ....

b. ....

c. ....

7. **How do you deal with emotions? E.g.**
    a. Able to acknowledge and express emotions
    b. Feel moved by a story or situation, the plight of someone
    c. Positive thoughts, appreciation, and gratitude

Your answers...

a. ....

b. ....

c. ....

8. **How do you relate to your feelings? E.g.**
    a. Always believe first impressions
    b. Gut instinct about position or people
    c. Able to relate to others in a crisis or difficult position

Your answers...

a. ....

b. ....

c. ....

9. **What do your beliefs say about you? E.g.**
   a. My thoughts become my beliefs, my beliefs become my actions and my actions dictate how I live my life
   b. Foundations of my principles
   c. Dictate my moral fibre - that makes me who I am

Your answers...

a. ....

b. ....

c. ....

10. **Where are you at with your goal setting? E.g.**
    a. Down on paper, in pictures, with a timeframe so goal setting is always in the subconscious
    b. Chunked into stages with rewards
    c. Birthing truck and antenatal truck for the mothers in my charity, Bega Kwa Bega (shoulder to shoulder), to be the clinic in the bush

Your answers...

a. ....

b. ....

c. ....

Look at who you are with all these fabulous traits and characteristics. Understand how you roll. Generate a philosophy that works for you. Apply your own personal philosophy to different areas of your life and just get started.

Now do all the exercises again.

This time, record the question and your own answers. Play the recording back. Listen to how you speak and articulate the words. Do they run together? Do you place any emphasis on any words? Do you start and stop words – dropping 'h's,' missed 't's' and 'd's' or inserting 'r's' before the letter 'w' in lawyer? Do you hiss, have a rasping vowel sound, or smack your lips together? Are you a heavy breather?

Set aside some time to practice your vowel sounds to improve the quality of the sound of your voice. Listen to someone who you believe has a real quality to their voice. How do they pronounce their vowels? Work at practicing words with vowels in them and imagine you are being presented to the King. You'd want to make a great first impression.

Record yourself each week. How is the sound of your voice improving?

Save the recording – it will be your benchmark for future comparisons.

SOUND

The 10 best questions to ask yourself about the sound of your voice of power

---

'When the whole world is silent, even one voice becomes powerful.'

— Malala Yousafzai

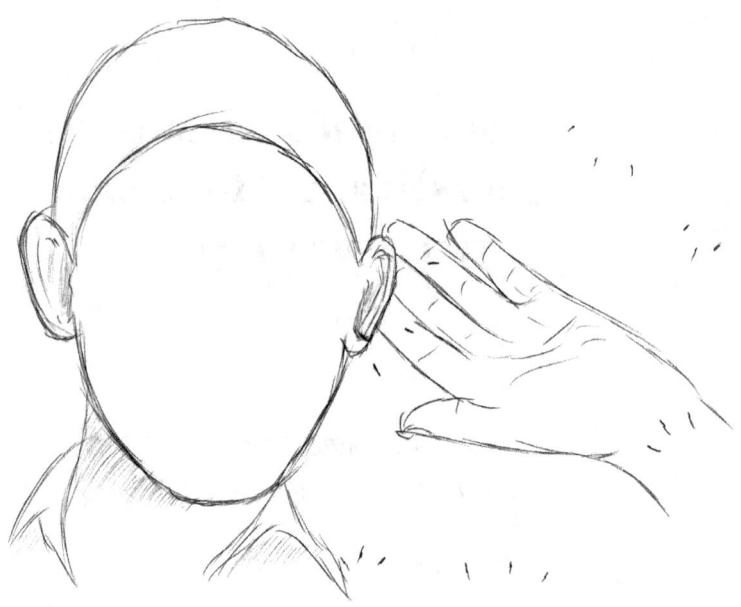

When was the last time you listened to a recording of your own voice? If the previous exercise was the first time hearing a recording of your own voice, then the sound of your own voice may seem strange. If 10 strangers were to listen to a recording of your voice, I guarantee that all would have different opinions of how you sound.

I had the privilege of working for a large media mogul for 5 years and I trained their clients to develop a polite voice. I recorded everyone and played each recording back for them. I never criticised anyone. I did not need to. Those who had a speaking voice that needed to be worked on, sounded rough in some instances. If you have spoken language traits, (I have a rasping Lanarkshire 'A' that needs to be firmly kept in check), then recording, or speaking in public with or without a microphone will accentuate any imperfections. The other joys are that if you do not finish your words, the words run straight into one another. People will find listening to you hard work. Also, if you speak too quickly, people can't understand your message or keep up with what you're saying.

A local radio station had a competition. Three celebrities were recorded saying one of the words of 'Who's on Heart?' The listeners were to guess the three names of the celebrities. The prize was £10,000 for one correct guess and £100,000 for all three. Many weeks passed before one celebrity was identified. The radio show published the celebrity names guessed each day on their website. A couple of months passed before the second celebrity was identified and almost four months later, one very lucky winner identified the third celebrity and claimed the £100,000 prize.

Clearly, we think we can carry the sounds of the voices in our heads, or maybe not with the thousands of guesses, notwithstanding the incentive of a very lucrative cash prize.

People can be very quick to point out our bad physical habits. Nobody ever tells us about our bad speech habits such as hissing (having a heavy 's' sound), deep breathing (usually inappropriate in a business telephone call), exaggerating words, running words into one another, speaking too loudly, quickly, or softly or speaking with a mouth full of food!

I skivvied in a shooting lodge between my junior and final honour's year. Everybody was called 'dawling' (darling to you and me), and the most interesting fact was that everyone knew when 'their dawling' was speaking directly to them. The lady of the manor said, "Remember Feeowna (Fiona), there's cashmere and there is cashmere." So too with voices!

Here are the 10 best questions to discover the sound of your voice of power. Write down the first three answers that spring into your mind as soon as you ask yourself each question. Then start practicing them by saying the answers out loud.

1. **Why do you need to sound confident, although you are not feeling confident? Listeners will:**
   a. Get to know, like and trust you
   b. Hear your confidence and conviction
   c. Be reassured that you sound professional

Your answers...

a. ....

b. ....

c. ....

2. **Why is sounding passionate essential? Listeners will:**
   a. Engage with you
   b. Feel your passion and resonate with you
   c. Share your story and join you on your journey

Your answers...

a. ....

b. ....

c. ....

3. **Why is it necessary to pace yourself when speaking? Listeners will:**
   a. Hear every word that you are saying
   b. Understand your message
   c. Interpret your message into a personal meaning for themselves

Your answers...

a. ....

b. ....

c. ....

4. **Why is it critical to get the volume just right? Listeners are:**
   a. Comfortable listening to you
   b. Able to concentrate without straining to hear your message
   c. Not overwhelmed by the loudness, therefore feel dominated by you

Your answers...

a. ....

b. ....

c. ....

5. **Why is pitch fundamental? Listeners will hear:**
   a. The quality of the sound of your voice, so you come across as pleasant and easy to listen to
   b. And feel the different atmospheres you create when telling a story
   c. How you portray a character, an attitude or emotion

Your answers...

a. ....

b. ....

c. ....

6. **Why use different tones of voice? Listeners will hear you:**
   a. Enhance the message and reinforce the meaning
   b. Demonstrate the different implications and suggestions
   c. Exhibit the range of your skills and abilities - warrior, sage, and lover

Your answers...

a. ....

b. ....

c. ....

7. **Why is it important to pause when speaking? Listeners will:**
   a. Connect what you are saying
   b. Interpret what you are saying into a way that is relevant for them
   c. Hear the emphasis on a particular word or emotion

Your answers...

a. ....

b. ....

c. ....

8. **Why would you elongate a word in a sentence? Listeners are:**
   a. Called to attention by your implication and effect
   b. Given time to catch up
   c. Changed by the change of emotion and even the state of the audience

Your answers...

a. ....

b. ....

c. ....

9. **How necessary is the flow of speech and, flow of a conversation? Listeners can:**
   a. Follow a logical sequence
   b. Keep up with you
   c. Understand the level that you are speaking at

Your answers

a. ....

b. ....

c. ....

10. **Why is it necessary to improve the quality of your voice? Listeners are:**
    a. No longer able to hear unconscious bad habits, such as smacking lips together before starting to speak
    b. Able to get more value from what you are saying
    c. Hearing you always confidently deliver your message

Your Answers...

a. ....

b. ....

c. ....

Now, I invite you to record yourself asking the questions and answering them. Play the recording back. Listen to how you speak. Do the words run together? Do you place any emphasis on any words? Do you start and stop words – dropping 'h's,' missed 't's' and 'd's' or inserting 'r's' before the letter 'w' in lawyer? Do you hiss, have a rasping vowel sound, or smack your lips together? Are you a heavy breather?

Set aside some time to practice your vowel sounds to improve the quality of the sound of your voice. Listen to someone who you believe has a real quality to their voice. How do they pronounce their vowels? Practice pronouncing words with consonants in them and imagine you are responding to the King's question: "Yes, Sir, it was a hard climb to the top of Ben Nevis with the snow, ice and the howling gale."

Or rather than repeat this same exercise from chapter 1, find out what you hear differently from the first exercise. Have you noticed any change in your speaking voice? What have you learned from doing another exercise recording your voice?

Record yourself each week. How is the sound of your voice improving?

Save the recording – it will be your benchmark for future comparisons.

3 SMILE

The 10 questions you need to ask yourself about your smile, stance, and stage dynamics

---

"You never get a second chance to make a first impression."

— Will Rogers

You are given that one opportunity to win over your audience, at the parent-teachers association; at a volunteers meeting; in a team meeting; with a management group; an important client; reporting to the board; representing your company at an event or selling services or products to a new prospect. Whatever the perception, whatever the pressure, you need to get your message across quickly. It must be clear, compelling, and above all, effective.

Your message must portray you as a confident and credible person. You need to use the mechanics of your voice to connect with your listeners and maintain their interest. The sound of your voice is your most effective communication skill for business.

This too, is also true in our personal lives How many times have you spoken on the phone with someone and well, you thought, 'delicious?' Does this ring a bell with anyone? Only to be so disappointed when the person turned up and was not on the top row of the chocolate box.

When you imagine a person's appearance based on their voice and sometimes how shocking can it be when you see them in person

When you engage with your audience, whether a single person or thousands, it is essential to be able to communicate at all levels. If your outcome is to raise interest or boost morale, the right power of voice and communication skills are required. Whether it is engaging with the employees on the shop floor, motivating sales and marketing teams or persuading stakeholders to lead and drive change, it is essential that you establish your own credibility. It is a crucial truth that it's never what you say, but it's the way you say it, that has stopped many budding leaders in their career path or broken a romance, before the first date.

The mastery of your voice of power is partially within the musicality of your voice, furnishing you with the ability to influence an audience. The more you use your voice of power to persuade and engage an audience to connect with you, the more fun that you and your audience will have. The more fun your audience has, the more likely they are to buy your ideas, products, and services.

The mastery of your voice of power is also about how you present yourself, how you show up and how you roll. You need to command the position of an expert, play that lead role in every move, and exude world-class star quality. You need to be comfortable being uncomfortable, radiate confidence, step up (regardless of what terrifies you) and above all, achieve.

Here are 10 great questions to ask yourself about why a smile can enhance your voice of power? There are tricks of the trade that keynote speakers use to enhance not only their physicality, but their stage presence, to make the experience more enjoyable for everyone. Here are some of the answers I came up with. Just say the first three answers that spring into your mind as soon as you ask yourself each question.

1. **Why does smiling enhance your voice of power? E.g.**
    a. Lifts your mood and raises your voice by an octave
    b. Makes the sound of your voice gentle, less harsh and more welcoming
    c. Projects your inner happiness

Your answers:

a. ....

b. ....

c. ....

2. **Why are our eyes important if the words are coming out of our mouths? E.g.**
    a. Your eyes are the mirror of your soul
    b. When the smile reaches your eyes, the smile is genuine
    c. When looking into the listener's eyes, you can see their reaction to your voice

Your answers:

a. ....

b. ....

c. ....

3. **Why is our eye contact essential? E.g.**
   a. Looking directly at your listeners means you are engaging with them
   b. Highlighting a point and pausing, emphasises when a word has more impact, if you look directly at the listener or a particular person in the audience
   c. Your integrity is enhanced when you maintain eye contact for a sensible amount of time

Your answers:

a. ....

b. ....

c. ....

4. **What are stage dynamics? E.g.**
   a. Using any stage or space to set the scene for your story, moving with purpose and conviction to relive the story in the present, through playing a character
   b. Changing where you are standing on stage, will separate the different phases of your story
   c. Experiment with different bodily positions - hands on your hips, tilting your head. Now speak with different facial expressions

Your answers:

a. ....

b. ....

c. ....

5. **How do you use the stage to your best advantage?** E.g.
   a. Going to the audience's left (your right), tells your audience that you are in your past – you can take on the persona of the characters and act the part
   b. Centre stage is being in the present, for narration and a position of influence to deliver powerful statements
   c. Going to the audience's right (your left) is going into the future

Your answers:

a. ....

b. ....

c. ....

6. **Why is your stance so important?** E.g.
   a. Your stance grounds you and gives you a presence when speaking
   b. It allows you to open your airways, breathe more deeply and relax
   c. It makes you appear more comfortable and more of an expert

Your answers:

a. ....

b. ....

c. ....

7. **What do you do if you are standing on a stage or a platform?**
   a. Never just stand still for too long. Use the area and a particular action that will demonstrate your point, e.g. hunch your shoulders
   b. When appearing in control, hold your hands in a neutral position in front of your body, or at your sides, but not in your pockets
   c. Use rhetorical questions, ask your listeners to agree with you - you can even tell your listeners to write things down

Your answers:

a. ....

b. ....

c. ....

8. **Why make up your own mantra or simply adopt someone else's?**
   a. To have words repeated to yourself for comfort and reassurance.
   b. A journey of a thousand miles starts with a single step, so repeating your mantra out loud or listening within your mind will keep you focused.
   c. Encouragement to remind you that you can do this

Your answers:

a. ....

b. ....

c. ....

9. **Why do you need to own the stage if it's a cast of one and not a thousand?**
    a. Vitally important to show self-worth, never appear arrogant, but with great humility. Royalty quietly enters, gracing us with their presence, always elegantly dressed for the right occasion and right on time
    b. Your family, friends, colleagues and sponsors will know they have made the right decision with you
    c. Listeners will feel your quality, bandwidth, sincerity and know what you stand for

Your answers:

a. ....

b. ....

c. ....

10. **Why is it necessary to be in control?**
    a. Radiate confidence that you are always the one-way, au fait with everything
    b. Shows your stability and being a grown-up
    c. Leadership. You can lead the audience while you stay in control

Your answers:

a. ....

b. ....

c. ....

Do the exercises again – this time record the question and your answers. Play the recording back. Listen to how you say the words. Do they run together? Do you place any emphasis on any words? Do you start and stop words – dropping 'h's,' missed 't's' and 'd's' or inserting 'r's' before the letter 'w' in lawyer? Do you hiss, have a rasping vowel sound, or smack your lips together? Are you a heavy breather?

Record yourself each week. How is the sound of your voice improving?

Save the recording – it will be another benchmark for future comparisons.

4

STYLE

The four different people types - never be at a loss for words again

---

'Formal education will make you a living; self-education will make you a fortune.'

— Jim Rohn

Imagine if you met a stranger in a lift and you had only two minutes to explain who you are, what you are doing and what your dreams are. How do you know that you are choosing the right words to resonate with him as your audience?

So, how do you recognise the different categories of people and how can you communicate effectively with them?

There are many ways we can recognise people types. Intellectuals for years have been educating us to effectively communicate through, e.g., Neuro-Linguistic Programming or Myers-Briggs. However, we do not always have the luxury or the time to study the person's behaviour or personality type, to find out how best to engage and connect with them.

We all like to be liked, but it is not so easy to like, understand or get to know someone in an instant. Remember, we never get a second chance to make that first impression. We make up our mind of liking someone (or not) within the first three seconds of meeting them. So, we stand a better chance of a win-win outcome if we understand the personality types.

Let's keep it simple. The easiest way to recognise people is to define them as four distinct character types – Red, Yellow, Blue, and Green. All four have easily recognisable traits and there are some distinct do's and don'ts, to make life easier for us.

The Reds – how to recognise them and the appropriate behaviours you need to demonstrate to effectively communicate with them:

- Individuals who are decisive, result-driven, and strong characters
- Can come across as forceful
- Impart robust guidance for whom they consider require it (willing recipients or not)
- Show dislike for those who fritter away their time

RED - DO TIPS	RED - DON'T TIPS
Be ready, willing, and able	Abandon things or status quo without options for what to do next
Pose detailed enquiries	Ask questions that cannot be answered
Be direct, concise and unambiguous	Use fluffy language or words with no meaning or direction
Stay with the matter in hand and don't get involved in idle chatter	Be unsystematic and higgledy-piggledy
Offer options and where doable, permit them to make the choice	Provide every single result and conclusion
Convince by putting forward points and outcomes	Being overly assertive

The Yellows – how to recognise them and the appropriate behaviours you need to demonstrate to effectively communicate with them:

- Party animals and lovers of social gatherings
- Enthusiastic and motivated by new ideas
- Wear their hearts on their sleeves
- Very passionate and imaginative
- Simply tire of something and easily side-tracked

YELLOW - DO TIPS	YELLOW - DON'T TIPS
Go out, meet people and entertain	Focus only on the details
Invite them to give their suggestions and proposals	Concentrate the conversation on day-to-day problems and concerns
Keep the conversation interesting and inspiring for them	Provide the best possible outcomes and suggestions for them to act
Be precise and exact	Command or decree
Ensure the contact is entertaining and enjoyable	Be aloof or unsociable
Keep the subject or topic at the highest possible level, don't drill down	Speak only of facts and figures

The Greens – how to recognise them and the appropriate behaviours you need to demonstrate to effectively communicate with them:

- Considerate and concerned individuals
- Open and honest consideration for others and their perspectives
- Would never hurt somebody's feelings
- Happy when everyone is engaged in all things
- Individuals and relationships mean the world to them

GREEN - DO TIPS	GREEN - DON'T TIPS
Be transparent	Be evasive or lacking openness
Pay attention and be approachable	Ignore the emotional content
Look for common ground	Compel them to action things in a hurry
Demonstrate honesty	Dive into business
Open questions to find out how they roll	Be curt or hasty
Be supportive and never quit	Drive predetermined conclusions

The Blues – how to recognise them and the appropriate behaviours you need to demonstrate to effectively communicate with them:

- Deal with facts, data, logic, and details
- Tend to be perfectionists
- Sometimes slow to make decisions, because they want to be sure they know what they want, before acting
- May appear overly cautious and not good risk-takers
- Feelings and emotions are kept inside and not revealed to others

BLUE - DO TIPS	BLUE - DON'T TIPS
Offer matter-of-fact confirmation	Be laid-back, familiar, or forceful
Cautiously put in plain words, why you oppose something	No coercive tactics
Put forward detailed specifications	Not completing a task or assignment
Give assurance and pledges when suitable	No risk taking or gambling with results
Be vigilant and relentless	Hang around
Identify positive and negative sides	Make unbalanced decisions

Once you have identified what type of person you are talking to, you will be able to tailor your conversation style. But remember, there is no magic formula. Always ask yourself, how would you like to be spoken to? More especially, if you were the customer, how would you feel?

The importance here is to realise that if for example, two Reds are head-to-head, then it will never be a win-win. The best position is to adopt some do's and remember the don'ts. So, the choice is yours – you just need to decide what your outcome will be.

I was the top sales consultant in several blue-chip companies, achieving many rewards. Selling is a far cry from years gone by. Now, we need to get into our customer's mindsets, as well as our own. Without knowing what they want us to do, think and feel, the win-win is beyond reach. No longer are we in a modern, fast-paced environment with only the customer's needs and wants. It is necessary to think about all our relationships – our family and friends, work colleagues, train buddies, folks at the gym and regulars at the local pub. We need to think of all these people as our customers too. When we acknowledge this, we can start to live the life of our dreams.

Our customers are everyone we meet for whatever reason. Our mindset and how we think is paramount. If we have the right frame of mind, then we can improve the quality of the words that come out of our mouth. That in turn greatly enhances the experience anyone who meets us will have. It is vitally important to set yourself above the rest and deliver a world-class customer experience, to ensure that your family, friends, colleagues, buddies and nodding acquaintances, will want more and return.

We need to always connect with our customers to solve their pain, problems, and issues. This is the best way to engage a world-class mindset:

- I am the Scottish Speech Coach (and for you, where the Scottish Speech Coach is mentioned, insert your own brand) to every customer
- My customers have faith that I will always communicate and keep them informed on progress of all objectives
- My customers trust me to help them resolve their problems
- I understand that every issue, no matter how small, is important to my customers
- I take personal responsibility for solving my customers' problems
- I am willing to step forward and stretch myself
- I work with my customers to stretch them, so they raise their game

WHAT I FEEL	WHAT I DO
I am proud to be the Scottish Speech Coach and love to show it	I do everything in my power to deliver what I promise
I am passionate about solving my customers' problems	I always work out my customers' problems and not share mine
I am always ready to listen to, and act on my customers' needs	I am always honest with my customers, even when it makes a conversation more difficult
Every time I am solving a customer problem, it is an opportunity to build their trust and loyalty	I take ownership for solving my customers' problems
I am an essential part of a team of experts, focused on maximising the potential of our business	I use all the systems at my disposal, to make the process as simple as possible for my customers

These are the capabilities and skills within your world-class mindset. I understand how to:

- See the customer as a person, not just their problem
- Find the root cause of my customer's pain
- Highlight what a great pain-solving experience looks like
- Maximise the potential of all available systems and resources
- Stretch myself and understand that my customers may be feeling stretched

It is also important to get into the mindset of your customers and this is what you want them to think. For me, I would want them to be saying, I use the Scottish Speech Coach:

- Because it is no problem to have a problem
- To fix my problems
- To get it right the first time
- Who will take the time to listen to my concerns
- To be there to help me

Then, we want to ensure that we know what our customers feel and do. This is what you achieve when you work in harmony with your customers:

WHAT MY CUSTOMERS FEEL	WHAT MY CUSTOMERS DO
I am respected for my opinions	I tell my friends and family how much I love working with the Scottish Speech Coach
I am listened to and understood	I express myself honestly, as I have faith that the Scottish Speech Coach, will deliver what she promises
I am engaged in a way that is right for me and my individual needs	I take any steps that are my responsibility, as I am clear on my own part of the process
I am comfortable in the solving process	I know that the Scottish Speech Coach, keeps me always informed.
I am impressed by the level of expertise, professionalism and care	I find every point of contact with the Scottish Speech Coach, a valuable experience

There are also the basics that your customers will expect you to do brilliantly. When a new potential customer approaches you with a problem or their pain that they want you to resolve, this is how they want you to behave:

- With complete focus
- Switched on and ready to help
- Show them that you are listening

This is how they want to be reassured when looking to use your services:

- Make it personal
- Polite acknowledgement of the state of affairs
- Reflecting the Scottish Speech Coach brand

When discussing the possibility of doing business, this is what they would like you to do:

- Give them time to talk
- Don't make assumptions
- Take their comments seriously

When confident that you have identified their problem, this is what they would like you to do next:

- Present a credible solution
- Make a mutual agreement
- Don't overload them with irrelevant information

When agreed that you have the right solution, this is how they want you to conclude the conversation:

- Summarise the agreement
- Explain what will happen next
- Say thank you and mean it

This is not a conclusive list, but a starting point to deliver that world-class customer experience, so your customers have your name on the tip of their tongue and give you the best, free and most influential advertising, by word of mouth or via social media. Simply the best!

SPIRITUALITY
It's within everybody

'I've learned that people will forget what you said, people will forget what you did, but people will never forget how you made them feel.'

— Maya Angelou

Spirituality is not only about religion, theology, or religious studies. It is about your very being and how you live your life. It is your faith, your beliefs, how you show up and especially how we interact with other people every minute of every day. This is not just about gifting to others, donating to charity, or volunteering, but being more generous in our actions and behaviour. A simple smile or kind word, stopping to exchange pleasantries or even just acknowledging people as we pass them in the corridor at work, is a great start. Remember, it's not what you say, but the way that you say it, that's important.

Part of this is living a healthier lifestyle. I do not need to preach, as we all know what we need to do - we only have one life.

We also need to focus on ourselves. Not retail therapy I'm afraid, but really reaching inside ourselves. Any inner exploration can be done through several spiritual disciplines such as meditation, prayer and journaling. Working on your breathing and being still, are great calming and control techniques for everyone and can be practiced anywhere. Speak to people, practice your voice of power and say uplifting things to others.

Adopt several daily mantras. Pick any of the following mantras to be the best in all circumstances and bring your own spirituality to life. Memorise at least 10 that are pertinent for you and repeat at least 5 times a day. Take your pick and add your own:

- I believe in me
- I am honest
- I am positive
- I am approachable
- I am knowledgeable
- I share my knowledge
- I am trustworthy and kind
- I am enthusiastic

- I share my enthusiasm
- I am a contributor
- I am a good friend
- I will encourage you
- I am fun
- I love to laugh
- I never give up
- I am gracious
- I am persistent
- I am here to help others
- I don't gossip
- I keep it simple
- I have big dreams
- I will succeed
- I will be there for you
- I will listen to you
- I will not give up on you
- I will work harder on myself, than I will on my business

We all have the necessary elements of success within us. These are in our thinking, subconscious mind, attitude, dreams, emotions and imagination. Creative visualisation was the catchphrase, so if you kept thinking about something, you would eventually attract it into your life. Now we refer to this as the Law of Attraction.

However, it is not sufficient to imagine your dream or goal for a few minutes, then spend the rest of your day full of fears and doubt. Seeing a particular thing, an occasion or certain circumstance in your mind, can cause you to attract it into your life. You need to have that burning ambition no matter what; you will do whatever it takes to accomplish your objective. You must use that immense power of your imagination and mental attitude, to persevere regardless of the setbacks. You must seize every opportunity that crosses your path and take massive action.

So how does this work? Our subconscious mind believes what we think and focus our attention on. This becomes a belief, and our subconscious changes our state of mind and thus our behaviours and actions. As a direct result, we meet new individuals, see other places, and enjoy fresh events. If our thinking is powerful enough, our thoughts will be unwittingly accepted by others, who can assist us with attaining our wishes and objectives.

We are all part of the universe and an inseparable part of the immense universal power. Our thoughts create energy and especially if emotionally charged, will alter the equilibrium, and invite transformation. For those who think, and the results end up the same, they need to change the environment they are thinking within. Think outside the box and choose a different location, people or desired end-result. You need to be very focused, explicit in detail and unambiguous about the desired goal.

If only 38% of what we hear are the words used, then a massive 62% is everything else.

Everything in life is in balance. It suggests the importance of moderation and equilibrium, emphasizing that a harmonious combination of different elements often leads to well-rounded and fulfilling experiences. This concept is often associated with the idea that finding the right balance in different aspects of life, such as work and leisure or responsibility and relaxation, can contribute to overall well-being and happiness.

Motivational speakers often use weighing scales to highlight balance. Often, they get us to imagine the different areas or parts of our lives, in blocks of different colours, sizes and shapes.

Then we must put the different blocks onto the two scales, in the hopes that the scales will balance.

I like the see-at-a-glance OXO-cube diagram with the nine squares. The reason I like the nine is because there are nine sectors in my life, and I can interchange them. The square in the middle is most important, because of the ramifications and interactions with the other eight. I can also distance some of the squares to work freely and independently so when I am there, I am assigning 100% of myself in person. When I am not, the world does not end, but allows me the freedom to take the time and energy to redefine the balance.

At any time, our focus can shift, as the internal walls are malleable which suggests that a particular thing or status quo offers flexibility or adaptability. It implies that the subject or existing state of affairs under discussion allows for changes or adjustments as needed to meet the requirements or objectives at hand. It also emphasizes the capability to respond effectively to different circumstances or demands.

Create your own OXO-cube diagram and fill in the boxes the areas/parts/sectors (call them what you like and are comfortable with), of your life that are important to you. You may realise that you have to move the squares around at different times or when things happen, to enable you to see all your responsibilities, hopes, dreams, activities and relationships.

This gives people the opportunity to focus on what is at the heart of their life.

Here is my OXO-cube diagram:

Sailing - pleasure, freedom, and relaxation	Health - diet, nutrition, energy	Scottish Speech Coach - keynote speaking
Sponsor children - charity trustee	Spirituality - faith, belief, prayer, meditation	Property - social landlord housing refugees
Family and friends	Exercise - walking	Contract work

So, how do we get that inner person out for the world to see and enjoy? Mahatma Gandhi said, 'Your beliefs become your thoughts, your thoughts become your words, your words become your actions, your actions become your habits, your habits become your values, and your values become your destiny.'

With this in mind, there are many benefits for you when you start using your voice of power to speak up and be confident:

- Talk from the heart
- Shine as a leader
- Own your own life
- Take up a lifelong opportunity
- Be pleased with your distinctiveness
- Make your own choices
- Embrace freedom
- Find like-minded friends
- Have self-belief
- Receive great recognition
- Lasting friendships
- Peace of mind
- Personal growth and development
- Realise your potential
- Recognition for your accomplishments and achievements
- Self-satisfaction

- Begin with no qualification
- Achieve things you never dreamed were possible to achieve
- Build your success
- Empower others to succeed as well
- Create a lifestyle for yourself and those you love
- Enjoy having fun
- Have hope for your future
- Unrestricted possibilities
- Make something from nothing
- Fashion a way of life for yourself and those you love

If spirituality is within, then surely there must be an A-Z guide on it.

A. Attitude of Gratitude – chance to make a difference, be ever thankful for all in your life

B. Blessings – for all the good things and miracles, no matter how small

C. Commitment – to your own success, plan your goals and don't stop

D. Dedication – to your dreams and aspirations, never let them out of your sight

E. Example – for all others to see regardless of how things stand, show your credibility and grit

F. Faith – to what you believe in, see everything as a learning experience

G. Growth – be an inspiration for others, a candle lighting the way

H. Hope – to all to achieve their wishes, with trust and reliance. Hope springs eternal

I. Inspiration – for others to keep going although the way is long and arduous

J. **Justice** – fairness and integrity when dealing with everyone
K. **Knowledge** – to make good judgement and to give to others
L. **Loyalty** – reliability, dependability and steadfastness
M. **Motivation** – to always keep going, no matter what
N. **Nurture** – those that need your help, sharing, succeeding and passing back
O. **Optimism** – in the face of uncertainty, overcome adversity and stay focused
P. **Passion** – for making a difference, a better tomorrow
Q. **Quit** – never an option, just start all over again with more conviction
R. **Risk** – all for your dreams, raise the stakes and do not stop
S. **Sacrifice** – de-clutter your life and dedicate to achieving your greatness
T. **Theology** – have that deep faith and belief that you will succeed, then give back
U. **Unselfish** – generosity of the heart and spirit to succeed
V. **Vision** – of where you are going and what you want to achieve
W. **Wisdom** – to always know the difference
X. **Xavier** – St Francis, set out on a remarkable series of missionary journeys
Y. **Yearly** – review of what you have achieved, re-set goals and aspirations
Z. **Zeal** – total determination to achieve the goal and live the life you have dreamed of

Live each day as if it were your last – you cannot go wrong.

STRENGTH

Super confidence and quiet strength - smile and think what you like

"You are as old as your doubt, your fear, and your despair. The way to keep young is to keep your faith young. Keep your self-confidence young. Keep your hope young."

— Dr L.F. Phelan

Experts tell us that the bumblebee should not be able to fly. Its body weight is too heavy, and its wingspan is too small, so in terms of aerodynamics, the bumblebee cannot fly. Thankfully, the bumblebee does not know this. So, if you don't know you have limitations, look at what you can achieve. Our only limits are the ones we self-impose on ourselves. We should never let our education put limits on ourselves.

We all know that our voice of power comes from within. How do we harness what is within and project it into the outside world, enabling us to achieve the life of our dreams? Firstly, are you where you want to be, or are you living in mediocrity instead of living with passion and excellence? If that is the case, you need to face up to the reality that you are not dreaming big enough – so big, that it is seriously scary. Have you set yourself a goal or a challenge in life recently? Have you cut out a picture in a magazine and pinned it up inside the front door (so you see it every time you leave and enter your home), and written a date of when you want to achieve it by? How fit are you? Do you ever walk instead of taking the car? Do you eat and drink too much? Just eat less French fries and have an extra glass of water, instead of the wine. Tiny consistent steps are all that it takes.

I dare you to challenge yourself! I also challenge you to write down three things at the end of each day that are marvellous, cheered you up, made you laugh, or you are grateful for. Then write down three things that you are going to do tomorrow to achieve your goal. If it truly is a big goal, cut it down into smaller chunks. Have you told absolutely everyone, so they can ask you about the progress when they meet you? You will be amazed at how motivational embarrassment can be. You will not want anyone to seriously think that you do not want to achieve your goal!

You have got to believe in yourself. Do not rely on anyone else telling you they believe in you. We have total control over our thoughts. We must nurture and affirm our self-belief in ourselves. We have our mantra to support us should we wobble. So, keep that self-belief as the uppermost thought in your mind. Turn it into action and continuous action will get you the results. Beware of the modern-day vampires who drain your goodness and energy. Cloak yourself in your beliefs and protect yourself by declaring them out loud. Do this daily or even hourly if needed.

When I was growing up, I thought you had to be someone great or significant to have values. However, we all have our values in the very core of our being. They are the essence of our thinking, and they make us the people we are today. We all know people who volunteer and are willing to give their time – that may be their purpose in life and it's great for the people who benefit from the gift of their time. When disaster strikes, we see the outpouring of people's core values – to help and support one another. Think about your core values and what they say about you. Do you live and breathe those values in every word that comes out of your mouth? That's a difficult one that also needs hard work and discipline every day.

Our outlook on life is everything – how we deal with the irritations, frustrations and let-downs. The great thing is that we can choose to have that sunny disposition. We can always say positive affirmations and repeat them. It's like getting into that moment of happiness and smiling – make that a habit too.

We should not just want something as a goal or an end-result, we should indisputably crave it more than anything. The powerful part is to be able to harness that desire. Commitment is paramount, but it can be positive and negative. It can keep us in our comfort zone, not willing to achieve greatness for fear of making mistakes or not being seen as the best. If you are truly committed to serving others, you will achieve great success. Commitment is the undisclosed ingredient for every recipe of success. On the other hand, achieving outcomes are deficient without learning a little or having fun. Success and achievement are more of the consequence of who you are and what you are saying, rather than what you are doing.

So, we can craft our voice to speak with influence and impact. The easiest way to get your 'ear in' is to listen to other speakers speaking. Listen and consider if you can hear any musicality in their voice. The best way is to listen to several short speeches – YouTube is a great source for you.

Ask yourself the following questions:

- Does the speaker speak with their hands?
- Does the speaker talk with a monotone voice?
- Does the speaker's voice get on your nerves?
- Do you know where you are within the story?
- Did you switch off and lose your concentration or did you hang on to every word?

Listen to several different speakers and find out what tones or qualities you recognise in their voices and start a list.

There are several components to super confidence and quiet strength, which you can practice. Here are the ingredients. The first is to speak with purpose. What your listeners will hear is your:

- Passion – the excitement, enthusiasm and even anger, if appropriate
- Power – the control in your voice, your energy and strength
- Positivity – sense your optimism, affirmation, and conviction

Second - practice your:

- Pronunciation – work on your articulation, accent and intonation
- Phrasing – your way with words and manner of speaking
- Projection - be heard at the back of the room, without listeners having to strain to hear you or be overwhelmed by the volume of your voice

Third - create your message, speech and beliefs, so your listeners will understand your:

- Commitment – pledge, dedication and steadfastness
- Conviction – confidence, sincerity and the principles you uphold
- Certainty – assurance, persuasion, and strength of mind

Fourth - credibility so that you will be able to: (Can these bullet points below all be on the one page)

- Communicate – convey your message, so the listeners share your beliefs
- Capture the Scene – if it says a thousand words, what will you achieve with it?
- Clasp – the listeners will see your authentic self and receive a personalised message

The bird said to the bee, "You work so hard all day to create the honey, and man comes along and steals your honey. Are you not sad?"

The bee replied, "Certainly not, man can only steal my honey, not the art of making it."

7 SHINE

Mastering the art of public speaking – communicate with clarity and charisma, captivating your audience – start exercising

'Exercise should be valued as a tribute to the heart.'

— Gene Tunny

Exercise used to be an unwelcome word - now it is part of our everyday lives.

A concert pianist will practice seven hours per day, seven days per week, for seven months, to deliver a one-hour recital.

Everywhere we are bombarded by the spoken word – good, bad and indifferent. Our auditory senses are assaulted daily by noise and sound, consciously and unconsciously. It is said that the conscious brain can only deal with seven to nine facts at any given time, but the subconscious is unlimited in what it can hear and store.

In the movie, The King's Speech, George VI (king of the United Kingdom) is helped to overcome a speech impediment, through encouragement and practice. In fact, it was Lionel Logue, an Australian speech and language therapist, and amateur stage actor who helped King George VI manage his stammer. His great ability to get King George VI to swear, was what caused the words to roll off his tongue. All great orators practice. There can be hundreds of takes when filming a movie to get it right. It may be that it is just an inflection on a word, to highlight the meaning and the emotion in the scene.

Sports professionals practice every day. Athletes start at the end of one competition to prepare for the next. It is cyclical. We too must practice our skills and perfect our voice of power.

When I was very young, I had elocution lessons. I would learn short sayings such as 'red leather, yellow leather,' 'the Leith Police dismisses us' and 'round the rugged rocks, the ragged rascals ran.' I would stand up in front of my elocution teacher and repeat each one 10 times during the lessons.

I then progressed onto poetry. William Wordsworth, *The Daffodils* was a particular favourite. I was able to convey such feeling and emotion with, 'I wondered lonely as a cloud that floats on high o'er hill and vale, and all at once I saw a crowd, a host of golden daffodils.'

Poetry is amazing to recite. The First World War poets such as Keats and Kipling, portray such drama and passion for their plight and present circumstance. Poetry is very personal. You may use poetry as a foundation to start exercising and recording your voice. It is essential that you choose a piece of poetry that suits your mood and temperament.

If you do not like poetry or if you are not in the mood, pick up a newspaper or a serious magazine and read it out loud.

Practice Exercise 1

- Read aloud from a newspaper or magazine
- Record your voice reading aloud for 10 minutes and then play the recording
- Be honest with yourself, how did you sound?
- Bring out the actor within you when you read aloud. Try different emotions, being happy, sad, with fervour, with aggression, even try putting an inflection on any of the key words in any sentence
- How do you feel? How was your performance? Would you dare ask someone to critique you – because Joe Bloggs sitting in the crowd will have his/her thoughts and opinions on what is good or bad? To be honest, it will only be their opinion
- Also, if you are at the front of the room delivering your speech, any inflection on your words, elongating words, emphasising words and pauses will heighten the emotion, and have an impact on what your listeners feel and how they react to your performance

Practice Exercise 2

The following are motivational sayings – each one is thought provoking. Say each one out loud. Then on the second run through, record your voice and once you have recorded all of them, listen to it and rate yourself from 1 to 10. 1 is the lowest (you do not like the sound of your own voice) and 10 is the highest, (you really like what you hear with no room for improvement).

- 80% of success is showing up - Woody Allen
- The mind is everything. What you think, you become - Buddha
- Your time is limited, so don't waste it living someone else's life - Steve Jobs
- Nothing is impossible; the word itself says 'I'm possible!' - Audrey Hepburn
- Remember no one can make you feel inferior without your consent - Eleanor Roosevelt
- I am not a product of my circumstances. I am a product of my decisions - Stephen Covey
- People often say that motivation doesn't last. Well, neither does bathing. That's why we recommend it daily - Zig Ziglar
- When everything seems to be going against you, remember that the aeroplane takes off against the wind, not with it - Henry Ford
- It's your place in the world; it's your life. Go on and do all you can with it and make it the life you want to live - Mae Jemison
- When I was five years old, my mother always told me that happiness was the key to life. When I went to school, they asked me what I wanted to be when I grew up. I wrote down 'happy.' They told me I didn't understand the assignment and I told them they didn't understand life - John Lennon

Practice Exercise 3

The following are excerpts from speeches. Say each one out loud. Then on the second run through, record your voice. Once you have recorded all of them, play it back and rate yourself on a score of 1 to 10. 1 is the lowest (you do not like the sound of your own voice) to 10 (you really like what you hear with no room for improvement).

- Steve Jobs, Stanford Commencement Address, 12 June 2005:

    Sometimes life hits you in the head, with a brick. Don't lose faith. I'm convinced that the only thing that kept me going was that I loved what I did. You've got to find what you love. That is as true for your work, as it is for your lovers. Your work is going to fill a large part of your life, and the only way to be truly satisfied is to do what you believe is great work. The only way to do great work is to love what you do. If you haven't found it yet, keep looking. Don't settle. As with all matters of the heart, you'll know when you find it. Like any great relationship, it just gets better and better as the years roll on. So, keep looking until you find it. Don't settle.

- President Barack Obama, Commencement Address Morehouse College, an all-male, historically black college Atlanta, 19 May 2013:

    So be a good role model, set a good example for that young brother coming up. If you know somebody who's not on point, go back and bring that brother along — those who've been left behind, who haven't had the same opportunities we have, they need to hear from you. You've got to be engaged in the barbershops, on the basketball court, at church, spend time and energy and presence to give people opportunities and a chance. Pull them up, expose them and support their dreams. Don't put them down.

So, it's up to you to widen your circle of concern — to care about justice for everybody, white, black and brown. Everybody. Not just in your own community, but also across this country and around the world. To make sure everyone has a voice, and everybody gets a seat at the table; that everybody, no matter what you look like or where you come from, what your last name is — it doesn't matter, everybody gets a chance to walk through those doors of opportunity, if they are willing to work hard enough.

- Richard Branson is a brilliant entrepreneur; not only because of his achievements, but mainly because of the culture he has created around each of his ventures.

  These are some of his sayings:
  - » You don't learn to walk by following rules; you learn by doing and falling over
  - » To me, business is not about wearing suits and pleasing stockholders, it's about being true to yourself, your ideas and focusing on the essentials
  - » My biggest motivation? Just to keep challenging myself, I see life like one long university education that I never had - every day I am learning something new
  - » My general attitude to life is to enjoy every minute of every day. I never do anything with a feeling of 'oh God, I've got to do this today
  - » Above all, you want to create something that you are proud of. That's always been my philosophy in business. I can honestly say that I have never gone into any business purely to make money. If that is

the sole motive, then I believe you are better off doing nothing
- » A business has to be involving, it has to be fun, and it has to exercise your creative instincts
- » Do not be embarrassed by your failures, learn from them, and start again.

- On the death of Princess Diana: Famous Speech by Queen Elizabeth II 9 September 1997:

No one who knew Diana will ever forget her. Millions of others who never met her, but felt they knew her, will remember her. I, for one believe that there are lessons to be drawn from her life and from the extraordinary and moving reaction to her death. I share in your determination to cherish her memory.

- Martin Luther King Famous Speech by Indira Gandhi, New Delhi, India, 24 January 1969:

They believed in the equality of all men. No more false doctrine has been spread than that of the superiority of one race over another. It is ironic that there should still be people in this world who judge men not by their moral worth and intellectual merit, but by the pigment of their skin or other physical characteristics.

- The famous inspiring speech, *Never Give In* by Sir Winston Churchill was delivered at his old school, Harrow on 29th October 1941. During the visit, Churchill listened to the traditional school songs and discovered that an additional verse had been added to one of them, in honour of this great man.

Another lesson I think we may take, just throwing our minds back to our meeting here 10 months ago and now, is that appearances are often very deceptive, and as Kipling says, we must '...meet with Triumph and Disaster and treat those two imposters just the same.'

You cannot tell from appearances how things will go. Sometimes imagination makes things out far worse than they are; yet without imagination, not much can be done. Those people who are imaginative see many more dangers than perhaps exist; certainly, many more than will happen; but then they must also pray to be given that extra courage to carry this far-reaching imagination. But for everyone, surely, what we have gone through in this period - I am addressing myself to the school - surely from this period of 10 months, this is the lesson: never give in, never give in, never, never, never, never in nothing, great or small, large, or petty - never give in except to convictions of honour and good sense. Never yield to force; never yield to the apparently overwhelming might of the enemy. We stood all alone a year ago and to many countries, it seemed that our account was closed, we were finished. All this tradition of ours, our songs, our school history, this part of the history of this country, were gone and finished and liquidated.

Very different is the mood today. Britain, other nations thought, had drawn a sponge across her slate. But instead, our country stood in the gap. There was no flinching and no thought of giving in; and by what seemed almost a miracle to those outside these islands, though we ourselves never doubted it, we now find ourselves in a position where I say that we can be sure, that we have only to persevere to conquer.

- John Fitzgerald Kennedy Inaugural Address, 1961:

  In the long history of the world, only a few generations have been granted the role of defending freedom in its hour of maximum danger. I do not shrink from this responsibility - I welcome it. I do not believe that any of us would exchange places with any other people or any other generation. The energy, the faith, the devotion which we bring to this endeavour, will light our country and all who serve it. The glow from that fire can truly light the world.

  So, my fellow Americans, ask not what your country can do for you; ask what you can do for your country.

  My fellow citizens of the world, ask not what America will do for you, but what together, we can do for the freedom of man.

Practice Exercise 4

Do these exercises for three consecutive days. Record the date at the start of each to differentiate the recordings. Go back and play them again. Ask yourself the following questions:

1. Have I read well? How good did I sound (rate each one from 1 to 10)?
2. What mistakes did I make? Did I stumble over certain words? When I repeated the exercise, did I make the same mistake?
3. Was there something that I particularly liked or disliked?
4. What would I improve on and why?
5. Did I sound melodious? Was I entertaining – even with the more serious speeches?
6. Did I put the right intonation on the right words – do I think the original speaker would have been proud of my efforts?

7. Do I sound good enough for television? If not, what do I need to do next – what do I need to improve on?

So, in words of one syllable, what you should be doing here is listening to your voice and if you hear a drawl, twang, brogue or burr, you have work to do. It is important to record and listen to the sound of your own voice.

Be honest with yourself. If your voice is working against you, no matter how much you know, you are going to fail. What would it be worth to you to fix that? Your voice can make you a fortune – speak out, it is a massive tool of influence.

SPEAK

Be in charge of what people say about you when you leave the room

---

'If you talk to a man in a language he understands, that goes to his head. If you talk to him in his own language, that goes to his heart.'

— Nelson Mandela

Be bold enough to use your voice, brave enough to listen to your heart and strong enough to live the life you've always imagined.

Communication is a form of art. For actors and presenters, their voice is the tool of their trade. I'd like to give you a series of little 'tricks of the trade' or tools that you can use and practice to sound like a professional speaker.

Traditionally, public speaking was standing in front of an audience or congregation and delivering some sort of dramatic monologue. Now we want to interact, interject, and even heckle to be part of the scene.

It is not always important to feel in charge, but to look confident and sound in control. That is what makes you more powerful and allows you to create the right impression. Using some of the tools below will allow you to be in charge of what people say about you, when you leave the room.

This is a series of my 10 top tips split into two main sections to guide you:

1. **All Eyes Are On Me** – 5 mighty tips to get over the fear of speaking in public:
   1. Being grounded

      It is so important to look confident and in control, even if you are shaking in your boots! The best way to impress anyone is to act as if you are in control. We all know how graceful a swan looks, gliding majestically over the surface of a lake. When the swan gets out of the water, they are cumbersome and never quite so beautiful when walking on land.

      To mirror that elegance is to be grounded. Stand with your feet firmly on the floor – it may be best to practice this in your bare feet. Relax and think about how comfortable you are. If not, slightly adjust your stance – move your feet until hip-width apart and you will look more natural.

2. Stand tall

   Pull yourself up, as if there was a string coming out of the top of your head and pulling towards the sky. Imagine that you are standing on the podium after just winning an Olympic gold medal. How proud would you feel? Think of your pose when you had the ribbon placed round your neck.

3. Put those shoulders up, down, and back

   Hunch your shoulders up, as high as they will go. Then force them down as much as possible. Then roll them backwards and stop. You should do these 3 exercises standing in front of the mirror, to see how your pose looks.

   Take a moment to look at how you are standing. Look at your pose and ask yourself how you feel about the way you look. Don't you look confident?

   If you were to deliver the inaugural speech as the President of the country, would you be impressed with this pose and the way you are standing? Would your pose tell the country, that you were the right person for the job and that you were in control of everything?

4. Take that important big, deep breath

   Breathe in through your nose and hold your breath. This may sound silly, but when we are nervous and anxious, we forget to breathe properly. Practice taking in a deep breath and holding it in for a count of 3. Then start to exhale slowly – first to the count of 4. Practice this at least 10 times. When you are able, take a deep breath, hold that breath for a count of three and then exhale to the count of 8. Practice this at least 10 times.

Look at your pose when you are breathing. Are you lifting your shoulders when you breathe in and dropping them as you exhale? Practice your breathing in, holding your breath and then exhaling. Always remember to keep your shoulders level.

5. Then, start to speak

   Those first words are what people will hear and remember. You never get a second chance to make that first impression. Practice the closing remarks and give your audience something to take home.

   It may be important to speak with fire and enthusiasm or from the heart, with passion. Always be in control and in tune with your message. Look halfway down the auditorium and when you start to speak, you will sound a little louder. It will calm your nerves.

2. **Speaking My Language** – 5 mighty tips to get your voice to communicate your message:

   1. Focus your attention

      Be prepared; don't agree to deliver a speech without adequate preparation or knowing who your audience is. It will be obvious. If you are asked a difficult question and don't know an answer, be honest. Never ask someone else in the audience to answer for you, unless with prior agreement. Bluffing will destroy your credibility forever.

      Do not swear – it may be funny, but it is impolite. Don't rise to the bait of a heckler, no matter what they do to provoke you. It will keep the audience on your side. Our audience is just like us. They too are not perfect. They just want to hear an unambiguous and transparent message, which is easy to follow.

2. Relax

Smile and when you speak, your natural sense of humour will prevail - leave the jokes to the comedians. Real life amusing stories are best kept short and should be used to link to the business theme of your presentation.

Remember you are delivering, not reading a bedtime story to get your audience to fall asleep. Why would your audience watch and listen to you, to only see the top of your head, as you stare down at your notes?

3. How do I sound?

We all have an idea of how we sound, but is it how everyone around hears us? Your accent gives you character and a unique quality of sound. A slight accent provides warmth, is distinctive and adds to your credibility.

A very well-known actor went to Hollywood, and he came back with no trace of his cockney (East London) accent. Recently, a Scottish couple were filmed encountering a bear in their suburban holiday home and the clip had subtitles! So, there are boundaries of what the brain hears and translates into understanding.

If you are going to use a microphone, check the volume. Speak up as it calms your anxiety and nerves. Remember, you can speak softly with heartfelt enthusiasm. You are also allowed to be enthusiastically silent.

Stay in the limelight. I went to hear a famous sailor, who had sailed around the world to speak. Her delivery was great, but she lost the audience because of where she stood. Remember, when using equipment, Murphy's Law says test is best.

4. Keeping up appearances

    No matter what you say, your clothes say more. When speaking to strangers, they do not know you. Keeping a suit jacket buttoned always appears more business-like. If unbuttoned, you will look more casual.

    Don't distract anyone with bling - irrespective of cost, it looks tacky. Dark glasses are for the Blues Brothers. The eyes are mirrors into your soul.

5. Practice, practice, practice!

    Practice the presentation or speech, until you can say it in your sleep. Remember, emphasise words and phrases, intonation, elongate words and pause. Don't forget to ensure that any actions or gestures coincide at the exact time, or it will look fake and badly rehearsed.

    Practice as much as you can, particularly with young people as your audience. Be prepared for the truth, they will be brutally honest, and it works best if it's interactive. Always pitch your speech on a level with the intelligence of the audience, irrespective of their level of knowledge and expertise. If your audience are anoraks, contrast and compare, do not use a specific level. That's what the handouts are for. The exception is in finance, when providing end-result figures.

    Time each paragraph. Make smooth transitions. Get on stage and know how you will feel – then practice your presentation visualising yourself on the stage. Video yourself, including any annoying habits or idiosyncrasies – we all have them. Never point a Pontius Pilate finger at anyone. For interviews, keep answers short and specific, to prevent misquotes. If you are camera-shy, just stay cool.

STORY

Easy as ABC

'There is no greater agony, than bearing an untold story inside you.'

— Maya Angelou

When Disney World, Florida opened, a reporter said to Walt's son, "It's too bad Walt didn't live to see this." His son replied, "He did, that's why you're looking at it now."

Disney is one of the greatest storytellers of all time. His credo was 'Think. Believe. Dream. Dare.' Disney movies are the real deal – such a complete package. If you follow his methodology for storytelling, then you will never go wrong. Walt's mantra was clearly to make his content special, not himself. If you make yourself as special as the storyteller, it will disempower you.

If you are in front of a live audience, input from the audience is paramount. If you watch any of the top comedians today, they always address the audience, especially those in the first few rows, directly making eye contact and usually heckling them as well – all part of the fun. Recently, a very famous comedian walked off stage, as a lady in the front row of the audience would not get off her mobile phone.

Top trainers often advise us to think of our audience as people in a restaurant – a hungry crowd to be fed. The first thing you want to do is build rapport with your hungry people. You want to paint a picture. Tell stories through pictures. Be specific about things, no ambiguity. The easiest way is to use metaphors or figures of speech, so they can interpret their own story in their mind with their own pictures. Only be very exclusive with your painting if you want them to have very individual pictures. Through humour, you can paint a very big picture. With any audience, pain is the biggest motivator.

To tell a story, you first must make a choice about the type of story it will be. Stories are best when they demonstrate vulnerability and imperfection. Stories need to be relevant to your message. As a storyteller, they need to demonstrate what compels you to take action, what you stand for and what has driven you to get to where you are today. Nobody follows an unscarred general, but you must look like the leader of the pack and be seen as the expert.

A great storyteller will not simply narrate the story. They may narrate a little to place the audience in the opening scene. Storytellers can then go into character mode and play the parts of the actual characters in the scene. The audience can have that first-person experience. The words the characters say, enable the audience to re-live the story, so that the scenes come alive. This moves the conversation, almost like a pay-day dialogue, with the audience across a coffee table. This enables the audience to get to know a little bit about the character. Here, the storyteller can be artful and creative in the words used.

Ideally, you are searching for similarities in your audience's world, so they can relate to what you are saying. It's a simple tap and transport into your audience's world with questions such as: do you remember a time when…? Or have you ever been in a setting when…? Use a metaphor or rhetorical question, to tap into every place so your audience gets to know, like and trust you.

If you are asking questions, you are investigating and keeping the audience interested. Characters can be described, so we don't have to figure them out which is the opposite of ballet, where you have the music and the dance, and you have to figure out what is going on. Our characters are our stars. They need to be seen. Great storytellers create an image in just a few words. What did he look like – did he look like George Clooney? I looked up to speak with him - rather than describing the character traits, simply address the character as Mr Bossy.

Our story should reflect our lives – it is our rite of passage. It is the journey of our life and from this, we can find and highlight themes. In a movie, there are always hints that imply certain things. Here, the dialogue tells the story.

There is always a struggle. Drama must have conflict. Soon it becomes obvious what the problem is, with the characters solving the problem. The inner dialogue of the character highlights the struggle to escape. The struggle highlights the difference in reactions over time. Conflict can be between two people, or it can be internal. Conflict may also be reluctance to make a decision. If it is a romantic story, then it centres on - will they, or won't they? If it is a thriller, then the hero gets there in the nick of time, our hero may be accepting or non-accepting, moving on in positioning from where they were showing the contrast.

Now we have our pivotal moment where there is a discovery. The scene has been set. We reach the summit. The characters show the audience what change has to happen and why the changes must be made. Words of wisdom come from the mouth of someone else. Perhaps, it is a child looking in the mirror and seeing the parent. There are many artful ways of reaching the pivotal solution. The solution is the result of making that fateful decision - what has happened as a result of that decision?

We experience a revelation previously not revealed. The hero usually has a phrase to sum up their beliefs, that we can quote in the key-clutch moment of life, but the result is different and close to the result you want. The seed has been planted - a thought or little sentence to summarise the message.

A story has three acts that can be summed up as Act 1 - State, Act 2 - Struggle and Act 3 - Solution.

In Act 1, the State, we find out who our characters are in the story. The audience finds out their strong points and their assets. In addition, what is of more interest, is to understand their faults and failings - that is why we can identify with them, relate to them and are instantly fond of them. We can understand their ambitions and their aspirations.

The additional side of this first introductory act is that we get to understand the state of affairs at hand and the subject matter, or what the topic or focus is. There is the introduction of the opponent, challenger or rival and we learn that they are the antagonist, adversary or maybe even a friend. The excitement is heightened by outside conflict or a peripheral disagreement, which always ends in defeat.

In Act 2, the Struggle, we see the main character in a state of bewilderment, perhaps misunderstood or uncertain on how to deal with a dilemma or predicament, therefore stays well away from it. The wise person or guru then appears and provides the channel or the vehicle, to motivate the reluctant hero into taking action – maybe as simple as a voyage or an expedition in pursuit of a mission. The task and the undertaking are made plain and understandable. Still, the reluctant hero is full of fear and trepidation, with real misgivings about the situation.

In Act 3, the Solution, the reluctant hero is in a real dilemma and his position gets trickier and difficult. He is forced to mull over and consider where he is at, in all of this and whether it fits with his beliefs and values. Then the skies clear and he sees the way forward as clear and transparent, and he is determined to do what is decent and true. If only life was so straightforward. More conflict, warfare and opposition come his way which he must rise above, defeat and triumph over. Our reluctant hero has changed – he has grown in stature, standing and is distinct.

The best way to produce great stories and perform them on stage is firstly to recite them. What is your most favourite Disney movie? Do you have the theme tune? Can you hum or sing it now? It doesn't matter if you don't know all the words. Start thinking out loud.

Exercise: Read each of the following questions for the three acts. Think about the answers. Set your stopwatch for three minutes for each act and speak for three minutes on each act, by simply answering the questions:

Act 1: What is the theme of the music? Where is the opening scene? Who are the main characters in the opening scene? Who is being themselves? What insight do you get into the characters, by their words and how they say them? Do you know who the adversary is or what the adverse circumstance is? What is the crisis? What has happened? What has gone wrong?

Act 2: Where are we at now? What are the issues and problems? What needs to be overcome? Who needs to do what? What is standing in the way of this being done? Are the issues real or imaginary? What is the turning point? Who is involved in making the shift?

Act 3: What else has happened? What is added to make the solution more difficult? How is our reluctant hero feeling? Do they know what they have to do? What is their light-bulb moment? What happens when they decide to do the right thing? What state do they have to overcome? What do they do to make things right?

Record each of the 3 sections – total recording time of 9 minutes.

At the end of the recording, ask yourself the following 5 questions:
1. How happy am I with the content? What parts of the story need to be improved?
2. What about the quality of my speech? Considering the individual components of my voice, what could I do better?
3. What tools, intonation, emphasising words, drawing out words, pauses, etc, could I use to enhance the story?
4. What emotions are apparent during the story?

5. How was the journey for the listener? Were they there for the duration? Was it a bus ride with people hopping on and off at different stops?

If you have never written a story and want to ensure you have captured the essence of the story, a great way to ensure you pick up all the vital parts, is to listen to a news story for 10 minutes. Do not write anything down. After 10 minutes, write the banner headlines. At the next news bulletin, simply listen again and tick off all the main points that you had written down. Practice this and you will become the best storyteller ever.

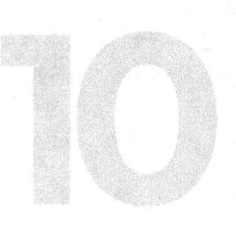

SPECIALITY
Re-invent yourself, give yourself a makeover

'Our deepest fear is that we are not inadequate; our deepest fear is that we are powerful beyond measure. It's our light, not our darkness, that most frightens us.'

— Marianne Williamson

If you do what you have always done, then you will always get what you always got.

So, how do you make a change? Just do it. Is it really that simple? If we want to be thinner, or more physically fit or want our hair to grow longer, then that will take time and dedication. We are our masters of our own destiny, but most people spend more time planning their annual holiday, than they do their life. So, can change really be so easy?

When you go on a journey, you need to know where you are going – what is your destination? Then you plan backwards or forwards, depending on your personality type. Some people sit on the train and face where they are going and some face where they have been. Maybe it is not even a conscious decision, just a force of habit.

So why are we afraid to be that shining light – be brilliant, gorgeous, talented and fabulous? Are we so self-conscious, uncomfortable, and shy of anything that sets us apart, that we don't want it? Really successful individuals recognise and understand their genius and talent. Maybe we need to take a leaf out of their book.

Have you ever experienced a life-changing situation, and your life has never been the same again, but you are still the same person as before? How did you feel? Did you grow up, feel like more of an adult, able to cope and surprised that you could deal with so much? Or maybe, you didn't have an option? You had been dealt that hand and you had to play to the end of the game.

Our life experiences mould us and make us the people we are today. But the million-dollar question is, are you happy, content and successful? Are you enjoying your life to the maximum and achieving all that you want? Or do you want more – or something else?

Use your most talented free gift, your voice, to create the life you have dreamed of. We live in our own minds. Our brain, intellect, and psyche, generate our thoughts which become our reality. So, if our feelings, opinions, and views manufacture our external existence, then we have the ability to control what is inside of us.

When we talk to ourselves in our own heads, we need to be hypersensitive and mindful, that we are feeding ourselves with the proper mental nourishment that keeps us well. We need to be the gatekeepers of our thoughts. We should be wary of fears, especially those that creep in and take over our emotions. Flashes of disappointment and failure can overwhelm a very successful day and leave us feeling emotionally impoverished. If there are instances when someone makes a derogatory remark that upsets us – we need to keep that in the moment and not allow any more time and effort to dwell on the negativity and its influence over us.

We need to be in our own mind daily doing proper housekeeping. What do I mean by that? For a start, are you kind to yourself? Do you say good, positive affirmations to yourself? No? Then it is time to start right now. Do you treat yourself as a star or do you feel that the limelight belongs to someone else? What makes a movie star stand out from the crowd? They are totally at ease with themselves, do not require any additional approval or require others to like them. We need to be more appreciative of ourselves, give ourselves compliments and tell ourselves that we know, like, trust, and love every bit of us. This may be a bit difficult at first, but with practice, all that knowledge, trust and love will shine out of us, and we will be a blessing to others with whom we come into contact.

It is great to read a motivational saying, but that is someone else's. Here are some examples of my own. Please write down 10 sayings that are personal and good for you.

- I understand my voice of power
- I have the courage of my convictions to speak out
- I have the passion to encourage anyone to listen to their inner voice
- I am passionate about working with anyone who needs encouragement
- I have the confidence to make the initial contact at any event
- I can share from my heart and give you the passion to get what you want
- I am confident that I am being listened to
- I am comfortable that I am getting my message across
- I create the right impression by what I say
- I take the stress out of speaking in public with practice and self-belief

Now your turn:

....

....

....

....

....

....

....

....

....

....

I had one of those life-changing moments. I wish I had carried out this following exercise a long time ago, but maybe it will help you on your journey.

At the end of your journey, what one line would you like to see on your gravestone?

Mine will read - Fiona loved life, and life loved Fiona. Live, laugh and love.

Yours: ....

Consider if your life was to end right now – what is your legacy to the world? How special are you? Have you done everything that would make a difference, or would you secretly feel that you had not done enough? If the answer makes you uncomfortable, you must look at your choices and decide.

....
....
....
....
....

Think of your best friend or someone you truly admire. What are the five things about this person (qualities, beliefs, principles, values, actions) that stand out to you?

....
....
....
....
....

If you were to be one famous person (movie star, hero, poet, astronaut, etc) who would you be?

....

If you stand back and look at all your answers, they will provide you with who you are, what you stand for, what you do to make a difference and what your star qualities are. It will give you the heart of your principles, beliefs and values and your purpose, beyond any goals that you set yourself.

Then, take the top 5 principles, beliefs and values and drill down what each one will give you. For example, if money is a prime objective, then it is not the actual money, but rather, what it can do for you. It is confidence and well-being that are at the core.

Next, write a wish list – if time and money were no object, what would be on your list? I had great fun writing down everything that I want.

....

....

....

....

....

Some of the perceived, most successful people, because of their lifestyle and trappings, are not necessarily the happiest or most fulfilled people. Most people focus on what they do not want. Focus on what you do want, revisit your wish list, and train your mind to seek out what is on your list; you will attract more of your wishes.

So, if some things are your absolute heart's desire, write a goal list with a timeline next to it. Don't write too many – top 6 goals and how long you think you will take to achieve them. Think about any hurdles that would have to be overcome, if they make the dream or goal unachievable, and then perhaps re-focus on a goal that is more attainable.

Also, think about what is around you – other people, resources and money may all be necessary to achieve your goals.

The most important part is to take action. Plan what you need to do and don't stop.

Remember to praise yourself and others and give rewards, as milestones are achieved along the way.

Draw breath, take stock, and ensure you are on the right path and your support is behind you.

Never give up. Just believe and have faith in yourself.

'Life is a game with few players and many spectators. Those who watch are the hordes who wander through life with no dreams, no goals, no plans even for tomorrow. Do not pity them. They made their choice when they made no choice.'

— Og Mandino

PART TWO

The Power of Your Written Words

Based on all the steps I used to write my book, and to avoid the mistakes I made including not publishing, I revisited the steps and created The Business Book Blueprint™. It is for business owners, who want to reach more clients, and position themselves as the go-to experts in their field. Also, to ensure that it would be easy for them, not only to write their book but make sure they publish their books.

I am working with business owners, to help them maximise their worth, and increase their value by helping others. It involves assisting them in establishing a lasting impact and creating a legacy by transforming their wealth of knowledge and expertise into the written form, through formatting and publication.

They can now call themselves authors.

Now you know why I am so passionate about helping others to become authors because in the last 10 years, I have realised that there are just 6 elements to writing a business book.

I would like to share with you the elements of The Business Book Blueprint™.

The Business Book Blueprint™

The Business Book Blueprint™

BUILD — The Raison D'etre Approach™

RECOGNISE — The Personal Positioning Principles™

IDENTIFY — The Successful Structure Framework™

DISTIL — The Get It Write Generator™

GENERATE — The Captivating Copy Method™

EVOLVE — The Lifeworks Legacy Maker™

To guide my clients in following the **B.R.I.D.G.E.** steps, I developed straightforward, highly effective strategies to support each of these six skill areas.

For **Build**, I developed **The Raison D'etre Approach™**.

What is **The Raison D'etre Approach™** and what do I mean by it? For you, it is literally the fundamental and essential motive you are writing your business book. It is a four-step process that enables you to capture your genuine deep and underlying purpose, so you have total clarity and direction to stay on track whilst you are writing your book. In simple terms, it will ensure you don't wander off topic.

Those aspiring authors who do not embrace **The Raison D'etre Approach™** discover that not only do they not connect with the real motivation they are writing a book, but the focus of the book is unclear, and they are constantly rambling off the point. The result is that the intention is hazy and woolly, causing the reader to quickly become disinterested, and eventually stop reading the book.

Moving to the second part of **B.R.I.D.G.E.** which is the ability to **Recognise** yourself, **The Personal Positioning Principles™** was created.

The Personal Positioning Principles™ ensure effective personal positioning, to help you stand out in a competitive market, attract opportunities, and make a positive impact on those around you. They are essential for building a strong personal brand, making a positive impact on your intensions for writing your book and building meaningful relationships with your readers.

By using **The Personal Positioning Principles™** you can articulate the value of your offer, what problems you can work out and how you can make a positive impact. You can also distinguish what makes you unique, sets you apart from others and highlights your skills, experiences, or perspectives, which make you different from your peers and competitors. Maintaining consistency in your personal positioning, your actions, words, and online presence will align with the image you want to convey. For you, this consistency builds trust and credibility, as well as strong bonds with your readers.

In contrast, those who do not use **The Personal Positioning Principles**™ can cause challenges for their readers to understand who they are, what they stand for and what they bring to the table, resulting in potential confusion and missed opportunities. Ineffective communication can hinder their ability to make a positive impression. Without a clear personal positioning strategy, their reputation may be shaped by others' perceptions and assumptions, rather than by their intentional efforts, leading to misconceptions or misinterpretations.

Moving to the third element of **B.R.I.D.G.E.** is the ability to **Identify**.

The Successful Structure Framework™ does exactly what is says on the tin. It enables you to **Identify** who your niche market is. In other words, it is a structured step-by-step process that helps you tailor your offerings to the right audience.

The significance is that it allows you to focus on your resources and ensures that your products or services meet the explicit needs of a particular group of consumers. Using it will also enable you to stand out and provide unique solutions, in a crowded market.

However, those who do not use **The Successful Structure Framework**™ have less effective marketing and decreased customer loyalty, because they are not giving their clients numerous benefits, such as enhanced product-market fit or improved brand resonance, because they are not tailoring their business approach to their chosen niche market.

So, you know why you're writing your book, and you know what you are an expert in. You now, in fact know who wants to read your book, who is really going to benefit from it and who is going to be a great client for you in the future.

The Get It Write Generator™ will enable you to **Distil** the most essential and valuable elements of your products and services, in several ways.

Individual clients and organisations learn in diverse ways. If you understand what suits them best, then you are far above the rest when it comes to distilling your wisdom and intelligence, to provide them with maximum benefit.

One of the easiest ways to understand how we learn and process information, is Gardner's Theory of Multiple Intelligences. Individuals and by default their organisation, possess various distinct types of intelligence rather than a single, general intelligence. These intelligences are linguistic, logical-mathematical, musical, spatial, bodily-kinesthetics, interpersonal, intrapersonal, and naturalistic. Knowing what style your clients prefer and how they relate to you, will also help the process of distillation.

Mind maps are another form of storing and generating information using words and images, to create strong associations.

The Get It Write Generator™ will enable you to **Distil**, collate, arrange in a logical order, and create an outline and structure that reflects your main ideas and relationships. **The Get It Write Generator™** will also distinguish and emphasise the core concepts, theories, or principles that are fundamental to understanding your area of expertise. In simple terms, you can process your major topics into a logical sequence that creates chapter titles.

In contrast, those who do not use **The Get It Write Generator**™ may not understand the need of condensing their knowledge. They may not break down information into core components and key concepts. Likewise, they may not establish a logical structure or outline, remove extraneous or irrelevant information, or express ideas in a clear and straightforward manner. In summary, they may not be able to effectively communicate and share their knowledge with others.

When you implement **The Captivating Copy Method**™ you are going to find that when you **Generate** your copy, it serves as a roadmap for your writing.

The Captivating Copy Method™ will ensure that the content of your book provides practical information, solutions and insights that are relevant to your target audience's needs and challenges. It will guarantee that it is written in a clear, concise, and reader-friendly manner. It will also include all the golden nuggets that ensure the book not only meets the needs but exceeds the expectations of the readers.

Those who do not use **The Captivating Copy Method**™ may not have created a cohesive writing experience. They may not empathise with the reader or enhance their own credibility. The most crucial point is that they may not understand their reader's needs, interests and pain points that will help them tailor their content to resonate with their readers.

The Lifeworks Legacy Maker™ ensures that as you **Evolve**, your book is a timeless means of preserving knowledge, ideas, and stories. It encapsulates the thoughts, experiences, and wisdom of you, as the author, ensuring it is accessible for future generations.

Those who do not implement **The Lifeworks Legacy Maker™** lose out on the opportunity to produce potentially amazing, life-changing work. Their work will never see the inside of a book cover, usually because they did not progress and did not know how to take it through to completion. They may also have the fear factor of pushing the button and publishing themselves.

A book can be a powerful and enduring legacy, which transcends time and continues to influence the lives of others. Your book, or business book can touch countless lives, shape conversations, and contribute in ways, beyond your imagination and wildest dreams.

2 B.R.I.D.G.E.

These steps help you to **B.R.I.D.G.E.** from the spoken word to the written word; to create a legacy from your wisdom that will be available to others, long after you have left the physical plane.

These six steps form the acronym **B.R.I.D.G.E.** to help you remember **The Business Book Blueprint™** more easily.

An acronym is a technique I have used to help you - you can use this for your clients to understand a new way of thinking, with a simple memory aid.

BUILD	RECOGNISE	IDENTIFY	DISTIL	GENERATE	EVOLVE

The first step in **B.R.I.D.G.E.** is to **Build** your objectives behind why you are writing your book and why it is important to you.

So, what does **Build** mean? For you, this could be something that lights you up, has intention, motivates, and energises you, gives you joy and inspiration, passion, interest, and enthusiasm, as well as being your goal, primary objective, and intention.

Once you have that real clear understanding in your mind about why you are writing your book and why someone else should read it, the next step is to **Recognise** your own expertise.

This step enables you to fully **Recognise** your own abilities, strengths, weaknesses, passions, and unique qualities. It is about how you are going to be distinguished and how you are going to be differentiated.

After you have built your why and you understand the recognition of your unique self, the next step is to **Identify** who is really going to read your book. Or in other words, **Identify** your target audience or your niche market.

Now, it's a matter of how you get that content down, in a way that gets it out of your head and onto paper. So many aspiring authors and great business owners get completely stuck when it comes to writing their books. They get that fabled thing called writer's block. They have got no idea what to write when they're presented with a blank sheet of paper - the only thing that comes out of their mind is blank ideas.

Remember the capacity of the human brain is vast and it can store an immense amount of information, throughout a person's lifetime. The next step in **B.R.I.D.G.E.** is all about how to **Distil** relevant knowledge and information that is in your head so that it is relevant for your target market.

Following that is the ability to **Generate** copy for a business book. You need to adopt a strategic and organised approach to writing content that effectively conveys your message and provides value to your target audience.

The final step in **B.R.I.D.G.E.** is to **Evolve**. Your book requires editing to ensure the content is clear, coherent, well-organised and delivers on your promise whatever your book promises to the reader. It also confirms consistency in language, tone, style, and formatting. Simple language means that readers can implement ideas and suggestions straight away, gaining immediate value and increasing your credibility as an author and a successful coach or implementer.

3 Build The Raison D'etre Approach™

BUILD

The Raison D'etre Approach™

We are going to deep dive into **The Raison D'etre Approach™**. This is where we're going to talk about our **B.R.I.D.G.E.** and how we **Build** with the end in mind and the precise steps we are going to take.

The four steps are **Reason**, **Reflection**, **Reach** and **Reality** for clarity, organisation, and ease of understanding. Breaking down **The Raison D'etre Approach™** into steps helps my clients follow a logical sequence and ensures that each component is addressed. This in turn will facilitate communication, education, and implementation.

Reason is the real reason you are writing the business book, the judgement behind your actions, developing the persistence or motivation of your choices and articulating the why behind your decisions. Your reason is your goal, your rationale, and your objective. However, if you are not clear about what your reason is, then you will not be clear about your intention, your motivation, and even your rationale. Collaborating with my clients, I undertake an exercise with them to really understand what is driving them and what the foundation that they are building on is so there is a solid footing on which to build their why and their motivation too.

Reflection, because it is so important to always pause and think about how far we have come. This is our progression from when we started to where we are, at this moment in time. The goal of your deliberation is to help your readers gain insights and guide them. Your aim is to ensure they apply the book's concepts to their own business or professional life. You want them to learn from real-world examples and improve their business practices. If you do not reflect, you will not be able to provide thought-provoking questions, self-assessments, or practical applications of the book's concepts which will help your reader build a better understanding of your theories and constructs.

Reach is the range and scope of your business. It is such an amazing exercise to undertake with clients. It typically refers to the extent or range of a company's influence, visibility, or impact. It can be measured in various ways depending on the specialised goals and metrics relevant to the business. Ultimately, increasing scope is a common goal for businesses aiming to expand their customer base, enhance brand awareness, and achieve overall growth.

When asked, if time and money were not an issue, what would be the scale of your business and where could you potentially take it? Thinking completely outside of the box and with no reigns to harness the magnitude of your potential, you can visualise amazing opportunities for you and your business.

Now we are going to start with **Reality**.

Why would we talk about **Reality**? In fact, what do I mean by **Reality**? It has got to be authentic. It is something that you have experienced. Now, here is something that is vital to know. Many of the entrepreneurs that I have worked with do not want to talk about failure. They do not want to tell anyone about it because they believe that it shows them as weak.

Now here is why this isn't true. Failure means that you are human. How can you ever be able to teach or encourage someone, if you have never had a failure or never had to get up off the floor? There is a famous Rocky Balboa quote, and you may want to remember this: 'But it ain't about how hard ya hit. It's about how hard you can get hit and keep moving forward. How much you can take and keep moving forward. That's how winning is done!' So, this is where people want to know what you did when things went wrong. Now, this is what is vitally important. If you had the same problem that they are going through now, they will know that you were able to get back up.

It is the failures and overcoming them to be triumphant that makes you more resilient. Those are the bits that people really want to read about. They want to read and understand the journey of failure to success. How was it, that you could take a circumstance as a failure and turn it into a position that is triumphant? If you look at all the great business leaders out there, the ones that we really admire the most are people like Richard Branson, Elon Musk, and the late, Steve Jobs. They all went from failure to triumph and triumphed spectacularly.

Understanding the **Reality** in your business, allows you to gain insights into the current state of your business, your industry and market conditions.

A SWOT analysis is a wonderful way to understand your business environment. It is a structured framework for assessing the internal strengths and weaknesses of your business, as well as the external opportunities and threats. This can provide a comprehensive view of the current authenticity of your business, and it can help you develop strategies to navigate it.

You remember Lesley, my client, the Sarah Davies lookalike of Dragon's Den, well, I had another client called Elizabeth, equally immaculately dressed and with determination to match. Well, about two years ago, Elizabeth invited me to meet her friend Rachel in a trendy coffee shop, in the heart of the city. Rachel was designer from top to toe and an extraordinarily successful business consultant in her own right.

Sipping her latte, leaning in with a grin, Elizabeth said: "You know Fiona, I've had my fair share of business mishaps. Remember my first start up - fantastic team and even some investors, but everything fell apart after one year. I was devastated."

An empathetic Rachel replied: "Oh no. What happened?"

Elizabeth said: "Well Rachel, I don't think it is a secret anymore. I overestimated my target market, didn't adapt to the changing industry, burned through my funding, so was forced to shut. It was as simple as that. I worked through the situation with Fiona. She made me take a step back, take a break, and re-evaluate my strengths and weaknesses."

Fiona then stated: "Elizabeth, you discovered your true calling and where you can make the most impact. What you said was that it taught you humility, perseverance, and the value of learning from your mistakes."

Now two years later, smiling, Rachel said: "Remember when I tried to start the restaurant; I thought being passionate about food was enough. It seemed like a great idea, but I was so naïve. It was a disaster - struggles with money, customer retention and competition."

Rachel replied: "Fiona, you taught me about strategic planning, customer satisfaction and understanding the market before diving in."

I concluded: "Well, Rachel, that's how you have been able to succeed in your consulting business, because your failed venture became a goldmine of insights. Breaking down the steps of the failures, gave you the stepping-stones of opportunities to enduring success."

Elizabeth and Rachel, using the **B.R.I.D.G.E.**, became very clear about the details of their failures and chunked them down to be something which more people can understand, and use inside their own business. They highlighted their actions within these significant steps. Using the techniques, they were able to write them down, making the steps logical to their readers, because they had gone through those same learnings and processes.

So, would you agree with me that people who see what you have gone through, and realise that this is what they are going through, will be able to relate to you and take confidence and conviction from your experience? I am sure that if you were sitting opposite me in a workshop right now, I would see you nodding, or showing me a thumbs up. I would even ask you to raise your hand if that makes sense!

4 Recognise The Personal Positioning Principles™

RECOGNISE

The Personal Positioning Principles™

So, once you have identified why you are going to write your book and why it is important to you, the next step is to **Recognise** yourself as the expert.

When you are regarded as an expert, this is when people will listen to you. They will also read about you, of course, because they will see you as the authority when you've written your business book. If you do not see yourself as the expert, your clients and potential clients will certainly not categorise you as the expert in your subject matter area. To achieve this recognition, I created **The Personal Positioning Principles™**.

The four steps are **Philosophical, Purpose, Premium** and **Performative**.

Philosophical implies some deep thinking about your expertise to reveal what it would highlight. I know each subject-matter expert has many recognisable sub-areas of expertise. The advantage of being philosophical is that it involves thinking critically, even about the basics and exploring different perspectives which will give you greater knowledge, you will be able to make more informed decisions and you will have a broader viewpoint.

If you are not philosophical about something, you may approach your subject matter area more superficially. You may not question things or explore alternative solutions or even think outside of the box to come up with a better answer or explanation. This can result in missed opportunities and limited perspectives on many things, such as saving money and time and being more resourceful.

Purpose is your determination, drive, perseverance, and tenacity. However, experts often feel pressure to conform to certain expectations regarding the rationale of their expertise. This external pressure can be at odds with the expert's true, authentic drive. Experts often have multiple roles and responsibilities. Society can place an overemphasis on external achievements, such as career success, wealth, or social status as the primary source of drive. **Purpose** is a highly subjective and individualised concept. What gives persistence to one person's life and expertise, may not resonate with another. For many experts, their commitment is a deeply personal journey. Their single-mindedness is what it takes to find an appropriate solution and see it through to the end.

So, everybody has determination. The reason I say that is because Viktor Frankl wrote a book while he was inside a concentration camp. Now, you might be thinking why anybody would even have steadfastness in that circumstance. Viktor knew his determination was to live. The fact was that he wanted to live, and he was not going to commit suicide. Viktor held on to the fact that he was going to see his family.

Premium is your exceptional quality. You are people's prime choice as the expert. They select you as being the best because your products and services are associated with high quality. Your clients may feel that your premium offerings are made with better materials, have superior craftsmanship, or offer exceptional performance. Your brand comes with a reputation for quality and excellence, which makes it seen as premium. Clients trust your brand to deliver products or services that meet exacting standards.

However, it is important to note that the perception of something as premium can vary from person to person. It is not based solely on objective qualities such as different criteria and expectations. Additionally, marketing, branding and reputation management can heavily influence the premium perception of a product or service.

Performative is the fourth step. To summarise step 1. **Philosophical**: define your underlying beliefs or principles by which you hold store; step 2. **Purpose:** clearly articulate the intended goal, objective and outcomes for your clients, and step. 3 **Premium**: single out and incorporate your elements of high quality, value, and excellence. So, step 4. **Performative** is applying your philosophical principles, commitment, and premium considerations to achieve the best and desired outcome for your clients.

Now if I were on stage speaking, I would say: Just being open and honest in this room, raise your hand if that phrase is familiar to you. I am not saying it's you, of course. But some people do not think they're good enough and that is because they're comparing themselves to the whole world. However, when I am talking about writing a book, for example, there are millions of publishers out there that achieve the aim of getting words into what we call a book.

We are not looking for a comparison with the entire world. We are looking for you to be the go-to person in an average size room of around 12 or 20 people. Would you agree with me, that you do not need to be the expert in the world?

You just need to get, perhaps 10 clients to begin with. So, think to yourself: Would 10 more clients be of use to me?' Of course, it would. Let us make it 9 clients because guess what? You are the 10th and you're the expert.

I collaborated with an amazing entrepreneur called James in the capital city. I was called and invited for coffee in one of those newly refurbished offices – you know the ones where you are always glad you wore your newest shoes and best business attire or suit, if you still wear suits today.

James' problem was that he did not think he was good enough. With the aroma of these Arabica beans, who was he kidding?

"Fiona, I don't feel I am the expert anymore. We were always getting distinguished for one thing or another. Always being mentioned in the financial pages of the national papers. Now, I feel like we are in the twilight zone."

"James, what was the last thing you got noticed for? Wasn't that about providing accurate information and promoting ethical behaviour?"

We worked through **The Personal Positioning Principles™** so James could see exactly where he was and what it was that he did daily. He followed the steps and at the end of each week, we had a review call. Within six months, James and his company had gone back into the top 10 businesses in his field.

James had not lost his place as an influencer or an expert anymore. He was back with a firm belief that he knew his stuff and it is just because I got him to reflect, pinpoint and talk about it. I got him to print out handouts and daily reminders. I got him to write a little book about each of his particular areas of expertise.

Here is a little exercise that I'd like you to do right now. I would like you to write this down. Please just grab a piece of paper.

You want to establish yourself as the expert in a room full of people. The best way is to be professional, respectful, and effective. So, how do you do that?

1. Write down 10 things (you may not need all 10) that you have a deep understanding of and know the latest information and trends about
2. What would your strong introduction be? What interesting facts or figures would resonate with your audience? Your qualifications, your experience, or any relevant achievements?

3. How would you encourage interaction with your audience? Questions, feedback, and opportunities for discussion
4. What could support you? Well-designed visual aids, not death by PowerPoint.
5. Actionable takeaways – is a practical application appropriate?

Remember these tips:
- Be confident, not arrogant
- Share your passion
- Provide references
- Follow-up – share your contact information with anyone who wants to learn more
- Have a genuine desire to help and educate others

You might want to remember this and even put this in your diary. You do not need to be an expert in the world, you just need to be an expert in your world. Please read this again. You do not need to be an expert in the world, you just need to be an expert in your world.

5 Identify The Successful Structure Framework™

IDENTIFY The Successful Structure Framework™

The third skill is to **Identify** who the ideal clients are that would need your expertise in your subject matter area. The solution I developed for business owners to name, distinguish, and understand this target group is **The Successful Structure Framework™**.

The four steps are **Specific, Solve, Situation** and **Systematic**.

Specific improves the clarity and depth of the explicit type of people who belong in your target or niche market. It highlights why they would need your goods or services. It also enables you to connect with them in a more compelling and meaningful way. As the expert, you will be able to provide clear, precise, and detailed information. Plus, it is important to have descriptions or examples of these individuals and their companies. If you do not have a clear and identifiable niche or target market, you will have a scattered approach trying to appeal to a diverse audience. This will make it challenging to create products and services that resonate with anyone.

Solve your niche market and it will enable you to make the necessary adjustments to your products, services, or offerings. This will make them more appealing to your target audience. In other words, what problems or types of difficulties can you sort out for these clients? This enables you to position your brand effectively, so it stands out in the marketplace. It makes your business and product not only unique but beneficial to your target customers. However, if you do not fully understand your niche market, you will not resolve their problems. Nor will you be able to build stronger relationships or address their needs effectively. Therefore, you will not be able to retain their loyalty and encourage repeat business.

Here is a little exercise that you can do for yourself and your business right now. I want you to write down all the problems that you know your clients are experiencing or have experienced in the past. Once you have written down all these problems and areas of difficulty, I want you to then highlight any that you could help them overcome.

Situation is knowing your niche market. It is key to creating tailored solutions, making informed decisions, and building strong relationships with your target audience. Regularly assessing and adapting your circumstances to meet the evolving needs and preferences of your niche market, will ensure long-term business success. You need to be constantly ensuring that your offerings provide solutions or benefits. Plus, you need to be addressing special interests, challenges and evolving solutions based on changing needs. This will ensure you are providing exceptional customer service, and value which will keep your clients coming back.

The one we are going to look a little deeper into is **Systematic**. So, what exactly do I mean by **Systematic**?

Would you agree that the belief is that all business owners know exactly who their target audience is? It is an old belief that business owners know who their potential clients are. However, some entrepreneurs are just serial business builders, rather than creating products and services that people want to buy.

The truth is that it is a mix of the two. If you are a serial entrepreneur, are you successful? How do you measure success? Is it by the number of businesses that you create or by the number of people you engage with who buy into your products and services.

You see, the biggest mistake that business owners make is not working out who their ideal clients are and how they can help them. In other words, their target audience inform them of what their key message should be (their selling point). Then they will know how they can help their ideal clients.

The impact is that although they may have a message that they want to convey, it may not be relevant and dependable, because they have not effectively identified their niche market and clients. Only then will it be the correct or ideal audience that they should be selling to.

For example, if you do not have a goal and a destination, how will you know when you will get there?

Here is what I want you to do. I want you to write down all the pain that you know that your niche market has. Now, at this stage, if you do not know who your niche market is, then I need you to go back to the previous step and work out who you're going to serve. This means that in **Recognise**, you need to have worked out exactly where you are an expert. I want you to go back to the exercise in the previous chapter, where we got to look at what you're an expert in and how you match with your ideal clients or niche market.

So, now you will know where you are an expert and what your client needs, because this is the problem you are going to resolve for them.

Let me tell you a story about one of my clients. I worked with an incredible lady, Claire, who was an expert in multi-level marketing. The thing was, Claire wanted to help everyone. Claire could help everybody, and she was right. She had a system that could help everybody, but the problem was getting to all those people. The thing is when we start talking about marketing, that's a different conversation because if you're talking to a man, you probably will have a different conversation than when you're talking to a woman. There will also be a different conversation if you're talking to a man who's in his 60's, in comparison to a man who's in his 20's. So yes, your system may be able to help everybody but here we are really niching this down to confirm where you are an expert.

You can help your clients because you understand their problems and pains so that you can get your marketing right. When I work with people on a one-to-one basis, we bring all these elements together so that they can determine exactly where they can help clients and work out issues.

If you think about the number of people who set up multi-level marketing businesses, research shows on average, they will get involved with at least 11, until they find their true niche. These facts have been identified by the big top 25 multi-level marketing businesses. If you consider Claire, she set up 7 multi-level marketing businesses and still never found her niche.

Claire loved **The Successful Structure Framework™** because she knew exactly what types of clients she wanted to work with. Claire fully understood that her clients' problems were really their fears. Once she could connect with their problems, she was able to work out ways she could work with them, to overcome their fears. Claire was very aware that those clients who had wants were really looking for her to provide them with a solution, because those clients wanted a way out or an alternative route. Claire was also very aware that when they had a need, they really wanted her to provide the benefit of the solution.

I worked with Claire to follow the formulaic process, **The Successful Structure Framework™** to the letter. As a result, she has had more consistent success in selling herself, than the 7 multi-level marketing businesses. Claire wanted tailored solutions and we found a way for her to talk with her clients, so they knew she was always talking to them directly.

Today we all know what an avatar and a persona is. Now, sometimes people think this is a blue cartoon character. Or if you are old enough, a Smurf, but it is not any of them. I think it is a good idea to have an avatar in each of our areas of expertise. Why should you have an avatar in each one of these areas? Simply because in each of your subject matter areas, your clients are not 100% the same. I knew Claire's clients had slightly unique needs and wants. So, we worked together to be able to address all those needs and wants, ensuring she had happy customers.

However, never more so than in this changing world, we need an avatar for each of our areas of expertise. Claire worked that out in our discussions early on. She worked out all the scenarios of each one of her different type of clients' problems, wants and needs so she had many solutions ready to hand when she met with her various clients.

6
Distil The Get It Write Generator™

DISTIL

The Get It Write Generator™

Being an expert, over time you would have gained a phenomenal amount of knowledge and information. However, when imparting information, it is important to strike a balance between giving too much and not giving enough.

The Get It Write Generator™ was created to help the business owner **Distil** all their knowledge and information into the realms of excellent know-how and learning. In other words, quality over quantity, to be able to practice crucial information management and decision-making skills regarding relevance.

There are four steps are **Gradual**, **Giving**, **Gain** and **Generate**.

Gradual is about your effective organisation and structure, which are crucial. Your book should follow a logical sequence, with chapters or sections that flow smoothly from one to the next. A measured approach is beneficial because it respects the learning process of the reader, taking them from a point of limited understanding to a deeper level of expertise or knowledge by the end of the book. It also reduces the risk of overwhelming the reader with complex information at the start and increases the reader's retaining and application of what they are reading.

Giving a solid foundation of essential concepts or principles before delving into more complex or advanced topics, will ensure your readers have the necessary background to grasp the later content. Also, providing a clear explanation of each concept or idea, breaking down complex subjects into manageable components and using plain language but avoiding jargon, will ensure your readers understand your information.

Your readers will **Gain** so much more by introducing real-life examples and case studies to illustrate the concepts that you are discussing. All your examples will help your readers see how your theory applies in practice. Your readers will also gain from practical exercises, activities, or application opportunities, to enable them to apply what they have learnt. These will reinforce their understanding and content and actively engage with you by undertaking the activity.

So many people think it is very easy to **Generate** content by simply putting words on a page, because you are the expert, and you know your content. However, you will want to ensure that this is not just what they are. Also, as you have identified exactly who your target audience is, you can tailor your writing to make contact with those people, in terms of what their interests are, demographics, preferences and how you serve them well. So, with them in mind, there are several key elements that will make your book not only engaging, informative and invaluable, but will address their needs, challenges and interests too.

As this is your book, you will be able to offer a unique perspective, approach and insight that will distinguish it from other books in the same category. It would be good to filter this knowledge down to say 10, 11 or 12 topics of your unquestionable expertise, which is a very readable amount. So, this will give you your chapter headings, plus an ideal framework to work with. Now, it is just a case of creating content, by literally filling in the blanks.

However, some aspiring authors think that they can effortlessly produce an entire book's worth of compelling and original content, in a matter of seconds, without any need for creativity or thought. This is not only absurd, but also a blatant disregard for the intricate and nuanced process that true business owners invest in, to produce meaningful and authentic works.

The truth is it is a combination of creativity, dedication, research, revision, and emotional investment. Writing a business book requires the exploration of ideas, careful consideration of themes, areas of expertise and a deep understanding of the intended audience. Business owners and experts often spend countless hours working on their expertise, revising drafts, and grappling with the complexities of experiences that not only inform, but entertain their readers too. The journey of creating meaningful and authentic works is a labour of love, driven by a genuine passion and a commitment to delivering something of substance to readers.

Your business book will highlight the key principles and strategies that contributed to your success, emphasising concepts that are meaningful to you and the importance of getting the right people onboard. You will be able to provide valuable insights into how your business transitioned from being good, to achieving sustained greatness.

Let us embark on the transformative journey of 'Elevate Your Business,' where we delve into a comprehensive and strategic exercise designed to enhance the stature and success of your enterprise. This undertaking is to empower your organization with the knowledge, tools, and innovative approaches essential for sustained growth and prosperity.

In the dynamic landscape of modern business, achieving sustained success requires more than just navigating market trends. It demands a strategic mindset, adaptability, and a commitment to excellence. 'Elevate Your Business' is your roadmap to not only surviving but thriving in the competitive business arena. If you can highlight to your clients how you navigated the sea of sameness to stand out, then you will provide a tried-and-tested route for them to follow.

Exercise 1:
The Ever-Changing Business Landscapes

Think about the rapid shifts in customer behaviour, new and emerging technologies, and the global trends that shape your business landscape. Think about all these underlying trends and how you understood them, so you were prepared to position your business for long-term success.

For me when I worked in broadcasting, it was about having a noticeably clear English accent. Clipped accents are no longer in demand. Now, it is about having a decent, local dialect. As much as being heard is important, it is about being able to be heard through blogs and videos. The written word is every bit as important as the spoken word.

Exercise 2:
The Power of Purpose-Driven Leadership

Look at the transformational influence of leaders, who have a positive impact on society and achieve long-term success. Think about business leaders in your area of expertise. Think about how they align their personal and organisational goals and what you did with yours to achieve new heights.

My earlier book was about *Discover Your Voice of Power* and now, this edition is about *The Power of Your Word9s* and to confidently share your wisdom. I help people not only to speak more fluently but to write better written words too.

Exercise 3:
Innovation as a Competitive Advantage

Innovation or improvement is a mindset that drives progress. Practical strategies for fostering a culture of innovation within your business and empowering your team to create new viewpoints, will enable you to stay ahead of the curve. Think about how you created your innovative mindset, by looking at how to approach issues differently, to come up with an enhanced decision.

No longer do people want to spend an interminable amount of time writing a book, or even a blog for that matter. This book blueprint is for you to complete writing your book in 12 weeks, which thankfully has been extremely well-received.

Exercise 4:
Building High-Performance Teams and Tribes

From recruitment strategies to nurturing collaboration in all different areas, your business will enable you to cultivate a profitable working environment. Think about how you have done this in all the areas of your business. No longer are we alone. We create collective environments for us to thrive. Time is finite, so non-repetition or duplication is very cost-effective.

For me, it is no longer one-to-one, but through the different mediums, it is one-to-many. With advancing technology, time differences are no longer a hurdle.

Lastly, chart your course to success.

Reflect on your deeper understanding of your business environs, your purpose-driven leadership, and your higher performance, which enabled you to stand out in the sea of sameness. These concepts, along with the practical exercises, any case studies, expert meetings, and consultations that you have undertaken, will enable you to showcase how you were able to elevate your business and navigate the ever-evolving challenges in the marketplace.

I have been able to contact clients 24/7 worldwide and became an international speaker through innovative technologies.

Remember, clients and readers learn more from your journey of failure to success. Failure is the one thing we all have in common. The tremendously successful people can narrate that journey with pride.

7 Generate The Captivating Copy Method™

GENERATE

The Captivating Copy Method™

The importance of copy, or written content, in a book cannot be overstated. The copy is the foundation of a book. It is what conveys your ideas, emotions, and narrative. There are several key reasons why copy is crucial in a book.

The Captivating Copy Method™ will help you **Generate** your copy. Creating appealing copy involves crafting text that grabs the reader's attention, resonates with them emotionally, and compels them to act.

The four steps are **Craft**, **Clarity**, **Compel** and **Call-to-Action**, often referred to by its short acronym, **CTA**.

Craft refers to the skilful and deliberate creation of written content to achieve unambiguous goals. Copy is both an art and a skill, requiring a combination of creativity, strategic thinking, and linguistic expertise. Crafting copy involves carefully selecting words, structuring sentences, and organising information to create compelling and persuasive messages that resonate with your target audience.

Clarity ensures that the crafted copy is clear and easy to understand. It conveys the intended message without ambiguity, ensuring that the readers grasp the information effortlessly. Effective copy is concise and to the point. Crafted copy eliminates unnecessary words and focuses on delivering the message succinctly, keeping your reader's attention. Business books are a medium for expressing business ideas. The quality of the copy determines how effectively these ideas are communicated.

Compel is highly significant in the context of writing copy because it encapsulates the heart of what effective copy aims to achieve. That is the power to persuade, captivate and drive the reader to take definite action. Compelling copy highlights what sets a product or service apart from the competition. It communicates unique selling points in a way that makes the offer irresistible. It also builds trust and credibility. By showcasing your expertise, providing evidence, or incorporating your testimonials, it convinces the reader that your product or service is worth their consideration.

Many writers, especially business writers believe that a **Call-to-Action** (**CTA**) is not a crucial element in writing business copy. They do not see it as the bridge between the persuasive content they have created, and the desired action they want their reader to take. However, many readers might be content with just absorbing information. The truth is that a **CTA** signals the transition from passive consumption to active engagement, helping the reader to distinguish between informational content and actionable steps. Without a clear directive, your reader may be unsure how to proceed or may not take any action at all. It tells them exactly what steps to take, reducing any ambiguity and making the conversion process smoother.

There is no right number of **CTA** elements in a business book, as it may vary based on the book's content, goals and overall strategy. While there is no strict rule on the exact quantity, it's essential to strike a balance. Too few **CTAs** may miss opportunities for your reader to engage, while too many can feel overwhelming or pushy. Consider the primary objectives of your business book. If the goal is to drive sales of a product, you may include limited **CTAs** related to purchasing. If it's about building an audience, **CTAs** for subscribing to a newsletter or following on social media might be relevant.

Focus on the most impactful actions that align with your business book's goals and avoid overwhelming your reader with numerous requests. Instead of repeating the same **CTA** throughout the book, diversify the calls based on the content. This keeps the reader engaged and offers different opportunities for interaction.

An exercise to see **Call-to-Action** statements or prompts, would be to include phrases that encourage action, such as 'visit our website,' 'subscribe now,' or 'join the discussion.'

However, think outside of the box to spot all the innovative ways to encourage potential clients to click on a link to give you their details. The categories may include exclusivity, urgency, emotional appeal, personalisation and interactive elements.

One of my authors, Roy, wrote his business book with the aim of bringing about positive change and guiding readers on how to implement his ideas presented. However, without relevant **CTAs**, Roy's book might have been perceived as informative, but lacking in actionable steps. The **CTAs** not only allowed him to leverage his book for marketing purposes, but they promoted related products, services and a series of new events. They were also instrumental in building a community of like-minded individuals. In other words, readers were able to connect and benefit from sharing their experiences and insights.

8 Evolve The Lifeworks Legacy Maker™

EVOLVE

The Lifeworks Legacy Maker™

The last and vital skill is **Evolve**. Business owners who have actively practised personal growth and continuous learning, make a positive impact on the people around them and the world in general. Such commitment to these ideals ensures they can create a lasting legacy, that extends beyond their immediate sphere of influence.

The Lifeworks Legacy Maker™ ensures its merit is not simply recorded but highlights how it extends beyond individual achievements and contributions.

The four steps are **Essence, Erase, Expand** and **Edit**.

Essence in the context of your business book, refers to the fundamental or intrinsic nature of any concept, idea, strategy, or principle about which you are writing. It encompasses the core elements or key attributes you have considered essential for your readers to understand and apply your business concept. For example, if you were referring to the core of your business strategy, you would most likely be referring to the fundamental principles or core components that make your strategy effective. It is about refining your concept down to its most crucial and impactful elements.

Erase means the importance of erasing mistakes, addressing inaccuracies, and refining concepts in writing a business book, cannot be overstated. Readers expect accuracy and reliability from a business book. Mistakes or inaccuracies can damage your credibility and undermine the trust of your readers. Erasing misprints, correcting inaccuracies, and refining concepts are essential steps in the process of writing a business book. It not only ensures the credibility and professionalism of your work, but also contributes to its long-term impact and success. A business book is a lasting piece of work.

Expand refers to the importance of thoroughly developing and elaborating your ideas. This is crucial in your business book because it helps ensure clarity and depth in your message.

Readers of business books often seek practical insights, case studies and a thorough understanding of the concepts being presented. When you develop your ideas, you must provide the necessary context, examples and details that make your content more valuable and actionable for your audience.

A business book typically requires a certain depth to cover topics thoroughly. This involves explaining different aspects of your subject matter, to offer a well-rounded view. The goal is to provide value to your readers. Whether it's through well-developed ideas, comprehensive contentment or both, broadening on your writing contributes to the overall quality of your business book. It enhances its impact on the audience.

Edit is a crucial step in the process of writing your business book and its importance is vital. Revising helps ensure that your ideas are presented in a clear and coherent manner. This is essential in your business book, where readers are looking for practical insights and actionable information.

Effective revising ensures that your message is communicated in a way that resonates with your readers, whether they are experts in the field or new to the subject. It helps maintain consistency throughout the book, both in terms of content and style, and is essential for building trust with your readers.

In summary, it contributes to the overall quality, professionalism, and effectiveness of your business book. It is an investment in the success of your work and its impact on your target audience.

However, many aspiring authors do not believe reworking is a critical step in the writing process that contributes to the overall quality, professionalism, and effectiveness of a business book. They do not consider it as investment in the success of their work and its impact on their target audience.

The truth is that a well-reworked book is polished and presents a professional image. This is important, not only for your readers, but also for potential business opportunities that may arise from the publication of your book. Effective rearranging may not always be explicitly stated but can be inferred from the overall reception and impact of the business book.

If the aspiring author has a positive reputation in the business community or within their industry, it may be indicative of the quality of their work, includes authoring of their books.

Editing your own business book can be challenging, as it is often difficult to objectively assess your own work. However, there are several exercises and strategies you can use to improve the revision process:

- Read your book aloud. This helps with awkward sentences, grammatical errors, and areas where the flow could be improved. It also allows you to hear the rhythm of your writing
- Develop a style guide for your book. Outline your preferences for spelling, punctuation, and formatting. Consistency is key in creating a professional and polished manuscript
- Share your manuscript with beta readers or trusted colleagues, who can provide constructive feedback. They may catch issues that you overlooked and offer valuable insights from a reader's perspective
- Pay close attention to details during the proofreading stage. Look for typos, punctuation errors and formatting

issues. It may be helpful to proofread your manuscript in multiple passes, focusing on different elements each time
- Break down complex sentences into simple ones. This not only improves readability, but also reduces the chances of any misinterpretation
- Create a checklist of common tasks and go through each item methodically. This ensures that you address multiple aspects of preparation for publication and does not miss the important elements.

An ambitious entrepreneur named Sarah, who attended my original business-book writing course, had accumulated years of experience in her industry. Recognising the need to share her insights and knowledge, she decided to write a business book to help others navigate the challenges she had faced and to provide valuable guidance for success.

As Sarah completed her manuscript, she understood the importance of proofreading and ensuring her message would be effectively communicated. Instead of rushing to publish, she embraced the editing process with diligence and patience.

After finishing the initial draft, Sarah took a break from her manuscript. This hiatus allowed her to detach emotionally and approach the revision process with a fresh perspective.

Sarah revisited her book with a focus on clarity and coherence. She paid close attention to the organisation of ideas, ensuring that her message was not only insightful, but also accessible to a wide audience.

Realising the impact a professional editor could have on the quality of her book, Sarah decided to invest in hiring an experienced editor. The editor helped refine the manuscript, offering suggestions for structural improvements, language enhancements and the fine-tuning of key concepts.

With the revision process complete, Sarah felt a sense of accomplishment. Her book was no longer just a collection of ideas. It was now a well-crafted, professionally-edited guide that would resonate with her target audience.

Upon publication, Sarah's book received positive reviews from readers and industry experts alike. The careful proofreading process had paid off, contributing to the success of her book in the competitive market.

Through her commitment to the editing process, Sarah not only shared her knowledge, but also left a lasting imprint on the minds of her readers, empowering them to achieve their own entrepreneurial success.

 **Ways to connect**

The key to successful connection is authenticity.

Be genuine, engage with your readers on a personal level and show appreciation for their support. Building and maintaining relationships with your readers is an ongoing process that can greatly contribute to your success as an author.

There are many ways to connect – here is a flavour of how we can work with you to connect:

Social media presence:

Platforms like LinkedIn, Facebook, or other relevant social media channels such as Instagram and X, allow you to share updates about your book, behind-the-scenes insights and engage in conversations with your audience.

Author of website or blog:

Your website or blog will serve as a hub for your work. Share information about your book, your writing process, and any upcoming events. Always ask for comments and feedback.

Book events and signings:

Attend book events, signings, and literary festivals. In-person interactions are incredibly valuable for connecting with readers on a personal level. Do take the time to talk to people, sign books and answer questions.

Online book clubs:

You could join or start online book clubs, related to your genre or exclusive to your book. Here, you will find the opportunity for readers to discuss your work, ask questions and share their thoughts. Do participate in these discussions whenever possible.

Email newsletter:

Create an email newsletter and encourage readers to subscribe through your website or social media.

Reader reviews and feedback:

Express gratitude for positive reviews and address any concerns or questions to demonstrate your appreciation for your readers.

Book launch parties:

Host virtual or in-person book launch parties to celebrate the release of your book. Invite friends, family, and your online community.

Collaborate with other authors:

Joint book promotions, cross promoting each other's work, or participating in collaborative projects, expands your reach and introduces your work to new audiences.

Personalised thank you notes:

Send personalised thank you notes to readers who have supported your work – it leaves a lasting impression and make them feel appreciated.

ACKNOWLEDGEMENTS

I want to say an enormous thank you to everyone who graciously helped me with their thoughts, enthusiasm, and wisdom, to create this book and share it with the world.

A special thank you to my sister Morag Anne Taylor for always being there.

To business guru, Lesley Campbell for the G&T, and the laughter. To *Find Your Why* Creator, Cheryl Chapman, for really believing in me and providing a platform for me to speak internationally.

To the technological experts, Reece Groves for the videography, and Ben Cook for photography and the original drawings in the book.

To the property ladies, Carole Ann Lyon and Narindar Singh for being an amazing support.

TESTIMONIALS

I love how open Fiona is to apply her greatest tools and techniques, to help people move forward towards achieving their outcomes, using their voice of power.

The quality of your voice is everything, whether you are a realtor or a coach. The old adage 'you only get one chance to make that first impression' is very true. It's not what you say, but the way that you say it, and the quality and the tone. All these tools can be used to improve your voice and make a big difference.

It's the voice, the words, and the overall sound when we use our voice, both internally and externally, that really drives our behaviour. As a coach, I can pick up on certain things through language and emphasis on certain syllables, to determine if someone is telling the truth, or if it is just a smokescreen based on how they speak.

The person with the most certainty and the most confidence can do anything and everything. The more they understand who they are and how they tend to show up, they can gain that confidence, really own who they are and make a big difference in them getting to their outcomes.

I really love how Fiona shows up each time. I applaud her for playing full out as always.

Trevor Douglas McGregor,
RESULTS COACH, ROBBINS RESEARCH INTERNATIONAL, INC.

I really appreciate what Fiona is doing with her book.

When you know what your end goal is and what you want to achieve, you only need to take small positive steps, you don't even need to take large steps.

A voice can be positive or negative, or even a bit in-between, but if you can use your voice properly, the difference you can make to someone else is amazing. There is an appropriateness that has to come with this and a responsibility and if you have both, people will listen. Communication and listening skills are the key to everything.

For people to communicate and for people to listen, there needs to be a connection. People portray who they are and what they are all about, through their voice. When people hear your passion and feel your inspiration, people will feel it too and share your journey. If you can hear the message, the learning will be greater.

Fiona's book will make you surely *Discover Your Voice of Power*.

John Brown
CEO LIFE SKILLS, DL VICE LORD LIEUTENANT FOR LANARKSHIRE.

Ways to connect with Fiona

LinkedIn
https://www.linkedin.com/in/fiona-taylor/

Facebook
https://www.facebook.com/fiona.taylor.7758/

Website
https://www.fmtcoaching.com

THE FAMILY

By Anonymous

The family is a little book,
The children are the leaves,
The parents are the cover that
Safe protection gives.

At first the pages of the book
Are blank, and smooth, and fair;
But time soon writeth memories,
And painteth pictures there.

Love is the golden clasp
That bindeth up the trust;
O break it not, lest all the leaves
Shall scatter like the dust.

www.ingramcontent.com/pod-product-compliance
Lightning Source LLC
Chambersburg PA
CBHW070118110526
44587CB00014BA/2044